A BOOK OF WITCHCRAFT

by the same author

A BOOK OF EPITAPHS
A BOOK OF SUPERSTITIONS
A BOOK OF PROVERBS

A BOOK OF WITCHCRAFT

by

RAYMOND LAMONT BROWN

*

With line whimsies by Ernest Petts

DAVID & CHARLES : NEWTON ABBOT

ISBN 0 7153 5174 5

Set in 10 point Plantin 2 point leaded
and printed in Great Britain
by Latimer Trend & Company Limited Plymouth
for David & Charles (Publishers) Limited
South Devon House Newton Abbot Devon

Contents

The Witch Defined

Ane witch be one that worketh by the Devil, or by some devilish curious art, either hurting or healing, revealing things secret or foretelling things to come, which the Devil hath devised to entangle and snare men's souls withal unto damnation.

George Gifford, 1587

A witch or hag is she which being (d)eluded by a league made with the Devil through his persuasion, inspiration and juggling, thinketh she can design what manner of evil things soever, either by thought or imprecation, as to shake the air with lightnings and thunder . . . and sometimes to fly upon a staff or fork. . .

William West, 1594

A witch is a magician who, either by open or secret league, wittingly and willingly consenteth to use the aid and assistance of the Devil in the working of wonders.

William Perkins, 1608

 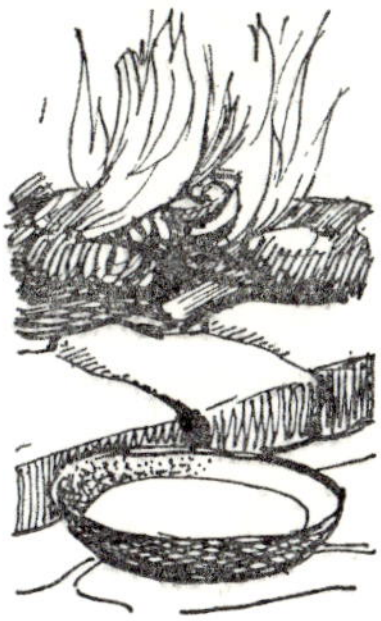 

I

Whence Came the Witches?

In a disused cemetery on Boa Island, County Fermanagh, Eire, among the hawthorn trees and bracken, where the ferns grow longest and the ubiquitous moss hides ownership of the mouldering slabs, there is a curiously carved figure of Celtic times, set like a squat dwarf on a pedestal.

Of pinkish-grey stone, the carved face, the predominant feature of the monument, stares with blank expression, open-mouthed and unblinking, towards the darkest shadows of this tiny graveyard. Those who stand for a minute or two in this eerie place, where no birds sing and no animals rustle in the undergrowth, soon imagine that they see the thin lips of that open mouth move in mystic whisper. To this stone, and the many sculptures like it to be found all over Celtic Europe over ten centuries ago, came those who had been chosen by their tribe to hear the wisdom and receive the directions of the gods. For in all ages and in all countries there have been men and women with a secret knowledge of the workings of Nature and the fashioning of charms and cures.

In his early environment, man's chief wants revolved around adequate supplies of food, shelter and clothing, and it was the task of these 'chosen ones' to perform the rites by which those needs might be satisfied. First among the ancient gospels of the magic arts would be the cult of feminism, for from the mid-ninth to the mid-seventh millennium BC, Europe saw the evolution of the matriarchal cult in which caves, woodlands and stars were all revered as female emblems. In that age, when men went out to hunt and women stayed at home to make medicine and magic, the myth of the Great Earth Mother was born and woman was hailed as her priestess.

Next in the scheme of things came the gods of the hunt, and man soon linked the chase with war and thence to death itself, as he began to believe in a two-tier creation of earth and paradise. Because they were beyond the credence of the simple, death and all the things not readily understandable were classed as 'witchcraft', although this term, when applied to early mystic practices, must have a connotation wide enough to embrace almost anything of a supernatural nature.

We saw on page seven how three early chroniclers defined witchcraft and witches, but modern researchers have found great difficulty in accurately defining something whose precise meaning has altered down the centuries according to the prevailing thought of the period. Dictionaries define a witch as 'a person who practises witchcraft, or magic; a magician, sorcerer, or wizard,' and go on, somewhat obviously, to define witchcraft as 'the practice of a witch or witches'. This, of course, is an over-simplification of the many aspects of witchcraft and unacceptable to the purist, who would regard 'witch', 'sorcerer', 'magician' and so on, as separate entities. As the contents of this book unfolds we shall begin to understand more precisely the subtle differences between magic, witchcraft and sorcery.

For a start, let us see how the early practices of fertility magic and pagan crafts developed into what might be called 'the delusion of witchcraft':

ANCIENT PAGANISM AND MAGICAL BELIEFS

REMAINED FOR CENTURIES AS LINGERING IDEAS WHICH GAVE SOME FUTURE SUBSTANCE FOR A SUPPOSED WITCH CULT

BUT WITCHCRAFT DID NOT BECOME ALIVE UNTIL ITS PRACTICE WAS MADE HERESY

DELUSIONS OF HERESY FOSTERED BY THE CHURCH BECAME THE BELIEF IN WITCHCRAFT OF THE PEOPLE

WHICH WAS LATER EXPRESSED AS A CONVENIENT EXPLANATION OF THE ILLS OF LIFE

And now to trace the process by which all this came about. From the idea that all women were potential magic workers there emerged eventually the belief that some women possessed more supernatural power than others. Thus, in time, one person would be singled out in a tribe as the resident 'witch'. Later, such supernatural powers were considered hereditary and the craft often became the prerogative of families.

Out of these community groups, it may be supposed, grew up sects like that of the Druids, whose faith was a form of state religion or worship centred on the king of the local tribe. Revered both as a god and as a priest, he was considered responsible for the fertility of the land, the people and their cattle; upon him devolved the task of providing hunting, fishing, bumper crops and fine weather by means of his occult powers. In a similar category were the priests of the Celts of Gaul, Britain and Ireland, who undertook to control the morals and religion of the people. In other places, however, there remained two types of 'witch': the herbalist charm-seller and the hereditary sorcerer whose descendant line again stemmed from the Stone Age.

Horned creatures, no doubt connected with early occult practices, are to be found carved or painted on rock, or on the walls of caves, at archaeological sites dating from 30,000 BC and spanning territory ranging from the Soviet Union to Spain. A good example is the Paleolithic painting known as the 'Magician', or 'Sorcerer' from a cave at Ariège, in France.

The early centuries abound in countless examples of the practice of witchcraft. It is recorded as being extant in Ancient Greece from the time of the poet Homer, c 700 BC, while the best-known sorceress of classical times is held to have been the legendary Medea, daughter of King Aeëtes of Colchis. From earlier centuries still the Egyptian chroniclers collated many practices which would today be deemed witchcraft; the long and involved funerary procedure of the Ancient Egyptians is almost pure classical witchcraft, and the world's earliest book, the Egyptian *Book of the Dead*, reads like a witch's secret treatise.

The famous Roman poet and satirist, Flaccus Quintus Horatius (Horace), left an elaborate description in *Satires* I.8 of the proceedings of two native witches in the Equiline cemetery:

> At the new moon they steal into it to gather bones and noxious herbs, their feet bare, their hair loose, and their robes tucked in. Making a hollow in the ground they rend

> a black lamb over it to summon the dead. They take two images of a larger one of wool (representing a witch) and a smaller one of wax (representing the person to be bewitched or punished). The moon turns red, hellhounds and snakes glide over the spot. Then they bury the muzzle of a wolf and a snake's tooth, and burn the waxen image.

Under Roman law, people were punished for necromancy and magic murder, rather than for practising any particular occult ritual. The earliest Roman law made the practice of magic a crime, but as the Roman world possessed a great deal of pseudo-medical lore, punishment only came when the practitioner was held to have acquired knowledge by occult means.

Biblical texts have frequently been quoted for and against witchcraft, and the injunction 'Thou shalt not suffer a witch to live' in Exodus xxii, 18, is an oft-quoted justification for their persecution. Modern scholarship, however, has rendered the Hebrew word *kashaph*, not as 'witch' but 'sorceress', or more properly 'poisoner', which is an entirely different matter. Factually, the Bible knows scarcely anything of true classical witchcraft, for even the few injunctions in the Old Testament refer to practices quite different from witchcraft. Modern research has further shown that the so-called 'witch' of Endor is nothing of the sort (1 Samuel xxviii); now translated as 'woman that hath a familiar spirit', the woman of Endor was clearly a spiritualist medium.

Throughout the centuries, whenever man has felt inadequate to cope with life he has turned to the supernatural, and the rise of the Dianic Cult was a typical example of this reversion to mysticism in time of need. Twin sister of Apollo and the goddess of chastity and hunting, Diana seems a strange choice as mediator for witchcraft, but through her association with the moon, she was deemed to have a darker side to her character. Called by many 'Triformis' and represented sometimes with the heads of horse, dog and boar, Diana was given a triple benefice:

as Luna she was the moon in heaven, as Diana an earth deity, and as Hecate she presided over the infernal regions, second only to the great god of the underworld, Pluto. In her Hecate guise, Diana was believed to possess great powers for enchantment and for turning bad fortune into good, and so was fervently petitioned by the credulous. St Paul's Cathedral, in London, is thought to occupy the site of a temple of the Dianic Cult.

Some researchers believe that much of the witchcraft practised by African tribes of today can be traced back to the influence of Ancient Egypt. While studying the witchcraft of the Zande of the Bahr-el-Ghazal, E. E. Evans-Pritchard was able to record (*Witchcraft, Oracles and Magic among the Azande*, Oxford, 1950):

> If blight seizes the groundnut crop it is witchcraft; if the bush is vainly scoured for game it is witchcraft; if termites do not rise when their swarming is due and a cold useless night is spent in waiting for their flight it is witchcraft; if a wife is sulky and unresponsive to her husband it is witchcraft; if a prince is cold and distant with his subject it is witchcraft; if a magical rite fails to achieve its purpose it is witchcraft; if, in fact, any failure or misfortune falls upon anyone at any time and in relation to any of the manifold activities of his life it may be due to witchcraft.

Not only does this probably sum up the Ancient Egyptians' conception of witchcraft, but the Zande are a northern tribe like the Dinka, Nuer, Mandari, Lugbara and Nyoro of the Sudan and Uganda regions, and it is well known that the Ancient Egyptians made several expeditions to the Sudan during the Early Dynastic Period 3100–2686 BC.

Mention of Africa at once suggests Voodoo (a West African corruption of the Yoruba word for 'god') but the association is invalid as Voodooism is definitely not witchcraft. Voodoo is the folk religion brought to Haiti by slaves from Dahomey (which became an independent republic in 1960). Incorporating elements of Christian ritual, and with a pantheon of Christian saints and African gods, the religion has also been influenced by various forms of European ceremonial and is still the religion of the majority of Haitians, despite efforts to suppress it. Its sinister associations date from the time when everybody believed in witchcraft. Voodoo worshippers themselves believe their religion to be a *defence against witchcraft*.

Looking back over the chronicles of the distant past, it can be seen that witchcraft, as it emerges into European history and literature, represents the racial memory of old palaeolithic magic cults supplemented by the 'magic idea' inherent in all known religions and various modern parodies of them. Thus, contrary to accepted belief, witchcraft may be said to be based on pre-Christian foundations, though never emerging as an *organised* religion. When Christianity came, prayers to God (perhaps accompanied by a miracle) took the place of such activities as rain-making, and the relics of saints replaced the wonder-working bones and charms of the early workers of magic.

In England during the Dark Ages, that long span between the departure of the Romans and the arrival of the Normans, *wicas* or 'wise-ones', adherents of the old folk cults that Christianity was slowly displacing, were to be found in all parts of the country. Little notice was taken of these 'witches' and if they were punished at all it was for turning the recognised magic arts (from herbalism to driving out evil influences) to mischievous ends. Throughout the early records there is an undoubted confusion between witchcraft and sorcery, so that before the late sixteenth century it is difficult to find any clear definition of witchcraft in England.

For many centuries in England Christianity was largely a matter of expediency, and pagan and Christian practices dwelt amicably beside each other for a long time. A blind eye was generally turned towards superstitious practices, and though the early priests and princes of the Church condemned superstition and magic (in 668 the Archbishop of Canterbury had ruled that people who socialised in heathen temples, or who wore the horns and masks of beasts while in mystic devotion, should do three years' penance), by and large the clerics had more important work to do in spreading the Gospel rather than in chasing after witches. Witchcraft, during the early centuries, was a crime committed against man rather than against God, and its punishment was much the same as that for any other anti-social act.

With the coming of the Middle Ages, when Christianity had gained a closer hold on all classes of society, witchcraft began to be viewed in a rather different light. The terms 'witch' and 'witchcraft', then began to have a more specific definition and the women 'old, weather-beaten . . . leaning on a staff, hollow-eyed, untoothed . . . mumbling in the streets', who probably officiated at a laying-out or laying-in with equal gusto, or supplied a cure for colic or ague from time to time, were deemed evil by the Holy Fathers, sniffing for any hint of heresy.

By the fourteenth century the Churchmen had succeeded in purging heresy from the ranks of the educated, and now turned their myopic vision towards the harmless but diversely odd rites among the humble folk which had previously been tolerated. Witchcraft was deemed a heretical cult, and remained so by limited definition for some three hundred years, loosely denoted as 1450 to 1750.

The ensuing war against heresy became an hysterical trauma and every disaster, natural and unnatural, had to have some sinister reason. Perhaps the most frightening occurrence, which was to unite Church and State against witches, was the Black Death of 1348–50. With one authority putting the death-rate of this terrible plague at about a quarter of the entire population of Europe, it was everywhere believed that God had sent this dreadful pestilence as a retribution for heresy. Many innocent folk, branded as witches, were to suffer in consequence.

In 1484 there came a piece of Church legislation which was to alter the whole attitude of authority towards witchcraft; in this year Pope Innocent VIII issued a Bull (so named after the *bulla,* or seal, affixed to the document) which condemned witches as people who were working widespread and organised harm against Christian communities. Thus were witches transformed from harmless old hags working herbal medicines to 'Soldiers of the Army of Satan'.

Anxious to be in the van for Papal approbation, two German witch-hunters, Dominicans Jakob Sprenger (1436–95), Dean of Cologne University, and Prior Heinrich Kramer (c 1430–1505), had published a book, *Malleus Maleficarum*—Hammer of Witches—which was to be used as a set book by inquisitors for centuries. In effect, the book presumed guilt at the outset and advocated torture and trickery to secure a confession of witchcraft. The persecution of witches became widespread in Europe; in one day 400 people were put to death at Toulouse, France, and 1,000 were destroyed in a single year around the district of Lake Como in nothern Italy. The coming of Calvinism only added to the impetus of the inquisition. No one dare speak out against the witch-hunters lest their pleas be taken as proof of partiality to witchcraft.

The hysteria was slower to arrive in England, where the particular domestic crises said to be caused by witchcraft did not provoke the requisite emotional fear. No such massacres of witches as those on the Continent took place but accusations of witchcraft were rife, and extended to all strata of society. Even royalty were not excluded; as witness the case of the English Queen, Joanna of Navarre, who had married Henry IV in 1402, and was accused in the Parliament Roll for 1419 of having 'compassed and imagined the death and destruction of our said Lord the King'. Although she was arrested, no evidence was produced and she was never brought to trial. But the incident was not forgotten and under the rule of Elizabeth I new laws against witchcraft were formulated making 'magical murder' and 'invocation of evil spirits' capital offences.

King Henry VIII, Elizabeth's father, took witchcraft far more seriously than had his more remote ancestors. Living in awe of witchcraft, superstitious Henry went so far as to believe that he had married the unfortunate Anne Boleyn because he had been seduced 'by witchcraft and that this was evident because God did not permit them to have any male issue'. As he grew older, Henry's fear of witchcraft increased and in 1542 he pressed the English parliament to pass an Act which penalised incantation, conjuring and witchcraft against a person's body, goods and chattels. Although from that date the authorities were empowered to act against witchcraft, no important witch trial took place until the first great English witch trial was staged in 1566 at Chelmsford, Essex, under an Act of 1563.

Elizabeth's successor, James I, a self-confessed expert on witches (Did we not write yon *Daemonologie*?), on his accession had passed a further Act providing the death penalty for 'any invocation or conjuration of any evil and wicked spirit, consult, covenant with, entertain, employ, feed, or reward any evil and wicked spirit to or for any intent or purpose'. Thus was the legendary 'pact with the Devil' first recognised in England.

In the punishment of witches, *organised* torture was never applied in England and no English witch was ever *legally* burnt or even hanged *as a witch*. When capital punishment followed a witch trial, the sentence was imposed for magical murder, or treason, or invoking evil spirits, and even then an offender was hanged (or strangled) before the cadaver was cremated. Ordinary sorcery was punishable, for the first offence, by one year's imprisonment and four six-hour periods in the pillory, with life imprisonment for persistent sorcery.

Although, as James I astutely pointed out later, Elizabeth's Act against 'Enchantments and Witchcraft' was an improvement on her father's enactment, it did not effectively punish witchcraft as a crime, taken as a whole. For Elizabeth's ministers, however, it succeeded in doing two things; it strengthened the law's arm in the persecution of conspiracy against the Queen (for there was scarcely a year in which the Virgin Queen was not subject to some clandestine activity), and it also served as a lever against any opposition to the new Protestant religion.

The period of the English Civil War, 1642–9, produced several testimonies of Royalists allegedly using witchcraft against the Roundheads (Oliver Cromwell's men) and vice versa, but though the Puritans still remained assiduous witch-hunters, the hysteria against witchcraft began to die out with the restoration of the monarchy in 1660.

From the records of witchcraft in England, seventeen cases emerge as major trials, each illuminating different facets of the laws and types of delusion:

First Chelmsford Trial, 26 July 1566. This trial against Agnes Waterhouse, her daughter Joan, and Elizabeth Francis, provided several precedents for later major trials, notably the acceptance of the uncorroborated evidence of small children, which was directly responsible for sending many senile old people to their deaths.

Dorsetshire Trial, 20 August 1566. Against John Walsh of Netherbury, Dorsetshire, whose replies to his interrogators reveal much *practical* witchcraft evidence.

Abingdon, or Windsor Witches, 26 February 1579. Shows clearly how the evidence of one witch (Elizabeth Stile, alias Rockingham) against other witches (Mother Dutten, Mother Margaret, or Margant, and Mother Devell) came to be a regular feature of later witchcraft trials.

St Osyth (St Osees) Witches, 1582. Rarely did a court of law permit such judicial licence to be taken as in this case.

The Warboys Witches, 5 April 1593. Singled out by many as the strangest of all English witchcraft cases, this was the trial in Huntingdon of the Samuels' family, a crone of near eighty, her husband and a daughter. For the first time in the history of English witchcraft, children were among the *accusers,* the trial being described as a true record of 'hysteria . . . ignorance, trickery, lies and imposture'.

The Burton Boy, 1596. Thomas Darling of Burton-on-Trent, Staffordshire, was said to have been bewitched into fits by one Anne Gooderidge of Stapenhill. Darling was the first of a number of boys to accuse innocent old women of bewitching them.

The Northampton Witches, 22 July 1612. The significant part of this trial of Agnes Browne, Joan Vaughan, or Varnham, Arthur Bill, Helen Jenkinson and Mary Barber, lies in the allusions to 'flying' and 'swimming' through the air.

Old Demdike and Old Chattox, 17 August 1612. The trial of these nineteen celebrated witches of Pendel Forest, Lancashire, is important for four main reasons. It was the first English mass trial in the modern sense; the gathering of the witches on the lines of a Continental sabbat was the first instance in English witchcraft; it involved a plot to rescue fellow witches from gaol; and it gives a clear picture of the development of certain witchcraft practices in the country districts since the passing of the 1563 Act.

The Bilson Boy, 1620. William Perry was the most celebrated of the imposters who claimed to have been bewitched; his imposture was discovered, however, and he was ordered by the judge to make a public apology; 'a true discovery of the late notorious impostures of certain Romish priests in their pretended exorcism. . . .'

The Newbury Witch, 1643. The strange case of a witch 'being overtaken by some Parliamentary Forces, as she was standing on a small plank-board and sailing on it over the River of Newbury'.

Witches of Faversham, 1645. A case involving the examination, confession, trial, and execution of Joan Williford, Joan Cariden and Jane Holt at Faversham, Kent. Perhaps its most striking feature was the testimony that the Devil presided over the meetings, and that a hedgehog was used as a 'familiar'.

Matthew Hopkins, Bury St Edmunds Trials, 1645. The classic story of England's most famous 'Witchfinder General'.

The St Albans Witches, 1649. A unique instance of an admission of the power of metamorphosis (in this case the ability of a human being to change into animal form).

The Anne Bodenham Case, 1652. The case of a witch accused of multiple metamorphosis—taking the guise of several animals.

Rose Cullender and Amy Duny, 1662. In this case the judge, Mr Justice Matthew Hale, allowed his own prejudices to lead him to accept perjured evidence and hearsay testimony.

Jane Wenham, the Witch of Walkern, 1712. The distinctive case of the Hertfordshire woman who was the last to be found guilty of witchcraft in England; she was reprieved.

Closer in spirit to the Continental attitude, Scotland persecuted witches with greater cruelty than in neighbouring England, for the Calvinists believed that evil was personified in the Devil (whose minions were witches) as firmly as did the Roman Catholics. Even so, there is no real evidence that many people were burnt alive in Scotland.

The ten main Scottish witchcraft cases worthy of the researcher's attention are:

John Fian and the North Berwick Witches, 1590. This trial had a direct influence on the witchcraft beliefs of King James VI and I and was an important event in the history of Scottish witchcraft.

The Aberdeen Witches, 1597. Witch persecution mania was here stimulated by King James's *Daemonolgie* and the result of the case affected a large section of the population, anyone who concocted herbal cures and natural remedies coming under suspicion of witchcraft. The trial caused a wider interest to be taken in the supernatural, especially among the 'wilder' Scottish lairds. Costs set out for this trial are of particular interest.

Isobel Grierson, 1607. Shows the first recorded breakaway from the old traditional methods of operation, although Scottish witches on the whole were much more imaginative than others in devising methods of torturing their victims.

Margaret Barclay, 1618. Indicates how deeply sunk in cruelty the Scots had become in the course of sixty years' of persecution of witches.

Perth Witch Trial, 1623. Shows the great attraction which charms and cures had over orthodox medicine, and how belief in fairies played a predominant part in Scottish witchcraft.

The Glenluce Devil, 1654. A poltergeist case (from the German idea of 'noisy spirit', a term used in Britain only after 1848) which resulted in the death of the witch who was charged with having been responsible for 'summoning' the manifestation.

Isobel Gowdie, 1662. Perhaps the case which reveals most about Scottish witchcraft beliefs, and contains one of the clearest references to coven and sabbat in either Scottish or English witchcraft history. The claims made by Isobel Gowdie for Scottish witch practice were the popular beliefs of the period. The case also shows what deep inroads Continental witch customs had made in Scottish witchcraft beliefs.

Thomas Weir, 1670. A clear case of the accused being completely insane, and indicative of the injustice of Scottish trial procedure in cases of witchcraft even at this late date.

The Bargarran Impostor, 1697. Represents to the history of Scottish witchcraft what the Warboys case does to its English counterpart.

The Pittenweem Witches, 1704. Shows how the Church of Scotland's bigotry fanned the flames of persecution, inciting mob violence.

Janet Horne, 1722. The last Scottish witchcraft victim.

During 1736, the 1604 Act *Anentis Witchcraft* was repealed and Scotland's law concerning witchcraft brought into line with that of England, but belief in witchcraft died hard in Scotland, if it ever has.

In Ireland, as in Wales, witchcraft never really became a major issue and little more than half a dozen cases of any note are recorded during the period from the first trial of 1324, when Lady Alice Kyteler was accused by Bishop Richard de Ledrede of Ossory of heretical sorcery, to the last trial in 1711, of a witch-poltergeist of Magee Island, near Carrickfergus, in Co Antrim.

King Charles II of England was not interested in witches and the last recorded hanging for witchcraft took place in 1684. In 1736 the 1604 law against witchcraft was repealed, twenty-four years after the last witch had been found guilty in England. The last to be *charged* with witchcraft were Jane Clerk, her son and daughter in 1717 but the jury rejected the indictments. Thereafter, the offence was to *pretend* to be a witch (sorcerer, fortune-teller, or fairground charlatan) for gain, but the fear which had lasted for several centuries could not be eradicated overnight by Act of Parliament and surreptitious witch duckings in the village pond continued for long after.

2

The Making of a Witch

The theory has been advanced that witches were needed as scapegoats on which men and women could release their hatred and fear of the society in which they lived. Hence, it is said, the archetypal 'old witch', an ugly old crone upon whom men could vent their pent-up wrath against the all-powerful Earth Mother, and women could bait for the ugliness they feared for themselves with the ravages of time.

Be that as it may, it is perhaps probable that certain people first became useful to a community because they appeared to possess some psychic or clairvoyant power. Later, either through fear or envy, or because some sought to use their power for evil purposes, these 'wise women' came to be regarded as 'witches', calamities instead of benefits were placed at their door, and some would be forced by torture to confess to having been the cause of such disasters. No doubt, too, a number of 'confessions' of witchcraft were prompted by some degree of masochism on the part of the victim, or even an inferiority complex which expressed itself in a need to be recognised by a community whatever the consequences.

All these ideas, then, played a part in the transformation of men and women into witches, but perhaps the most important factor, so far as women were concerned, lay in the inferior position to which they were relegated in medieval society. Denigrated by the Church, the easy playthings of the feudal lord and his vassals, and often the animal-servants of the men in whose household they dwelt, small wonder that women were apt to turn for protection to the old cults and to the spirits they believed were all about them.

And what a variety of cults they had at their disposal. Every tree, flower and stone was thought to have its attendant spirit, all of which, together with other 'familiars' of hearth and home, had long been objects of superstition. To a woman pushed to the edge of dementia by starvation or cruelty, folk superstitions could take on the delusions of reality. The old custom of placing a saucer of milk for the fairies by the hearth to encourage them to help with the household chores would soon come to be regarded as an essential tribute to a protective 'spirit', but by observers as some sinister rite for invoking the powers of evil.

As suspicion grew, and the unfortunate woman began to fear for her safety, she might be driven from her home into one of the woods or forests which, in the early centuries, covered much of Europe like a mantle. When she had learnt to live on roots, herbs and berries, she would master woodcraft and begin to study and understand the secrets of nature. Or perhaps she might choose to live in a cave or hut made from wattle and daub, her only companions being the creatures of the forest, or maybe a stray cat or dog. And as she sat at eventide with her pet in her lap, talking to it in loneliness, those among the common folk around who might venture to pass and peer at her through the undergrowth would see her as a terrifying creature and her cat as the living embodiment of evil, only a step away from a witch and her familiar spirit, ripe for all manner of evil.

In his *Faerie Queene*, Edmund Spenser (1552–99), put into verse the popular idea of the witch, which remained in the mind of the people for centuries:

> There, in a gloomy hollow glen, she found
> A little cottage built of sticks and weeds,
> In homely wise, and walled with sods around,
> In which a witch did dwell in loathly weeds
> And wilful want, all careless of her needs;
> So choosing solitary to abide,
> Far from all neighbours, that her devilish deeds
> And hellish arts from people she might hide,
> And hurt far off, unknown, whomever she envied.

Some thirteen years later, in 1603, Samuel Harsnett, Archbishop of York, gave the clerical view in his *Declaration of Popish Impostures*:

> Out of these (impostures) is shaped (for) us the idea of a witch—an old, weather-beaten crone, having the chin and her knees meeting for age, walking like a bow, leaning on a staff; hollow-eyed, untoothed, furrowed on her face, having her limbs trembling with palsy, going mumbling in the streets; one that hath forgotten her paternoster, and yet hath a shrewd tongue to call a drab a drab. . . .

As belief in the powers of witchcraft grew from decade to decade, there was no lack of new recruits but many popular fallacies concerning the 'initiation' of witches. A common delusion was that the Devil introduced himself when the victim was alone. In the guise of a human, he might accost a solitary walker, or appear as a disembodied voice while the victim lay abed. Initially it was supposed, the Devil inquired about the prospective initiate's personal troubles and, having shown his power by remedying them, demanded in return that his new subject should renounce God. Once having done this—a truly traumatic step to take in ages when the two-tier system of Heaven and Hell was widely believed—the Devil's latest recruit was said to be able to rely upon his personal tutoring in witch charm-making and divination, in how to dismember corpses for potency and how to spread disease.

The ultimate degradation and height of initiation was believed to be sexual intercourse with the Devil, and open 'admission' of this has been a familiar feature of witch trials down the ages. Finally, so that the Devil's own could recognise one another, a Witch's Mark was bestowed. At first these marks were usually held to be *polymastia* (extra breasts), or *polythelia* (extra nipples which appear along the line between armpit and groin) ostensibly to 'suckle ye devil'. But as trials for withcraft became more and more frequent, any abnormal growth was taken as the Devil's brand of identification.

The supposed rituals of initiation into witchcraft have become somewhat confused with the passage of time. Even today, amongst those who practise witchcraft derivations, the form of initiation differs from coven to coven, and from country to country. All, however, would appear to have something in common with the rituals of sexual initiation which, from time immemorial, have had both social and magical importance. In the Amazonian regions of Brazil, for instance, there is a sexual initiation of young girls among the Takuna Indians. Called *Moça Nova* (in Peru and Colombia, it is called *Pelazon*) the ritual is carried out when the young girl shows the first signs of puberty. After a six months' incarceration in a dark hut, her mother and grandmother being her only visitors, the girl is brought forth on the night of a full moon and, after a sequence of ritual sexual dances, is brought into the presence of a symbolic phallus. This symbol is also an indispensable part of most if not all, witchcraft initiations, though in some covens complete initiation was not achieved until the *Osculum Infame* was given.

This consisted of kissing the Devil (ie, the high-priest) on the buttocks.

Remembering that initiation ceremonies do vary from coven to coven, a modern initiation as a witch might take the following form:

For some time beforehand the neophyte witch will have received instruction in the witch mystagogy. Then, following a ritual bathing, she will be placed, naked and blindfolded, beside a specially cast circle. Having declared that she does not wish to change her mind, the ceremony begins with the witches present dancing around the inner part of the circle chanting or singing the 'Eko, Eko Azarak':

Darksome night and shining moon,
East then south then west then north,
Harken to the witches' rune,
Here I come to call thee forth.

Earth and water, air and fire,
Wand and pentacle and sword,
Work ye now to my desire,
Harken ye unto my word.

Cords and censer, scourge and knife,
Powers of the witches' blade,
Waken all ye unto life,
Come ye as the charm is made.

Queen of heaven, queen of hell,
Horned hunter of the night,
Lend your power unto the spell,
Work my will by magic rite.

Power of land, and sway of sea,
Might of moon and gift of sun,

Do as I will, and let it be,
Chant the spell and it be done.

Eko, Eko Azarak,
Eko, Eko Zamilak,
Eko, Eko Cernunnos,
Eko, Eko Aradia.

Standing at the votive altar in symbolic pose, with outstretched arms and legs to represent the pillars of life—trunk straight for the tree of vitality and arms for mercy and justice—the high-priest of the witches identifies himself by his secret name and recites the proclamation in Runic by way of preparation. Then, assisted by the high-priestess holding a sword above her head, he evokes the 'power' and turns to question the initiate, now bound arm and ankle.

Question: 'Thou who standeth on the threshold of the dread and ancient Lords of the outer space, hast thou the courage to make assay? (*The priestess touches the initiate on the left breast with the sword.*) For say I verily, it were better that thou rush upon this mystic blade and perish than to make false admission or attempt to enter with fear in thy heart.'

Response: 'I have two perfect words. Perfect love and perfect trust.'

Reply: 'All who have are doubly welcome.'

This completed, the high-priestess lays her sword on the floor, leads the initiate into the circle, embraces her and bestows upon her the witch name by which she will henceforth be known.

Still bound and blindfolded, but inside the circle, the initiate is led to each of the four cardinal watchtowers.

Once more the other witches whirl in a circle chanting, 'Eko, Eko Azarak,' to raise the 'cone of power', and at this point there begins the sexual and purifying ordeal, at which the phallic symbol is in evidence.

A circle cast for the initiation ceremony

The circle might contain:

A sword
A black-handled knife
A white-handled knife
A watchtower
Four candles for the cardinal points
A censer
A chalice
A pentacle

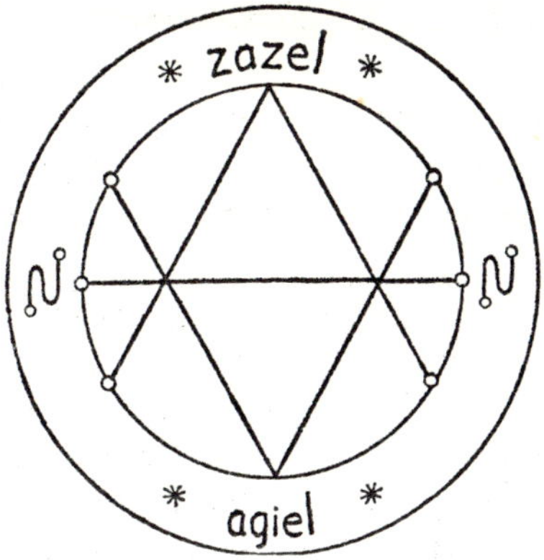

A pentacle for good luck at initiation

After ritual kiss-blessing on feet, breast, mouth and stomach, a ritual scourging usually follows, leading to the swearing of an oath of secrecy and loyalty to the coven. Next, the new witch is given the seven working tools of witchcraft: a black-handled knife (athame), a white-handled knife, a wand (to control certain 'ayngels' or 'genie'), a pentacle, a censer of incense, a scourge (the sign of power, dominance, purification and enlightenment), and the cords (to bind the symbols of witchcraft). Usually, a ritual eating of cakes and wine rounds off the ceremony, though in the United States, in the Ozark Mountain region of Oklahoma and Arkansas, it is said to terminate with the recitation of the Lord's Prayer backwards. Initiation into the higher grades of witchcraft is much more complex, involving ceremonies lasting several hours.

At a number of witch trials the fact that 'earthly initiation' could not be proved was held to be of no importance, the inquisitors maintaining that initiation could take place before birth. As proof of this they cited ugliness, and certainly they had some excuse if we are to believe an early chronicler's description of the birth of Ursula Southtell, later to be called Mother Shipton (the celebrated witch of Knaresborough, Yorkshire), from *The Strange and Wonderful History of Mother Shipton* (1686):

> The body was long, but very big-boned, great gogling eyes, very sharp and fiery, a nose of unproportional length, having in it many crooks and turnings adorned with great pimples.

Or again, as Henri Boguet noted in his *Discours des sorciers* (Lyons, 1602), children 'usually followed their mother's manner of life', so that the offspring of witches, it was said, were initiated during parturition. This belief in the hereditary possibilities of witchcraft was widely held in law and medical fraternities alike, and even used as evidence at witch trials; as Francesco-Maria Guazzo thus commented in his *Compendium Maleficarum*, issued at Milan in 1608:

> The infection of witchcraft is often spread through a sort of contagion to children by their sinful parents, when these try to find favour with their devils. For the greed of Satan was ever limitless and insatiable; thus, when once he has entered a family, he will never give up his foothold except with the greatest difficulty. And it is one among many sure and certain indications against those accused of witchcraft, if one of their parents were found guilty of this crime. There are daily examples of this inherited taint in children, for the Devil is always busy to increase the number of his adherents. And there can be no better way of attaining this end than by urging and compelling those who are already in his power to corrupt their own children.

In one of the latest manifestations of witchcraft, during the revolt against the Tshombe government in the Congo in the early 1960s, initiation into a coven of *dhawa* witchcraft involved the taking of oaths, drinking a potion made from *chanvre* (blue lotus) and avoiding all contact with women or white men, be it even the latter's clothing. In return, the initiates were assured of immunity from the bullets of the enemy.

3

Pentacles and Secret Signs

A circle is an important factor in modern witches' ceremonial for, according to their teachings, it is 'between the worlds'; that is, it marks out a territory between this world and the next in which mortals can communicate with spirits. Only the symbol of the circle really matters, and it may be marked out with chalk or paint or even with household objects. The circle, usually nine feet in diameter (unless otherwise prescribed for a special purpose), is drawn out before each ceremony with a consecrated magic knife. There are also usually two outer circles, each six inches apart, so that the total diameter of the area is eleven feet.

Once drawn, the circle is 'purified' by the high-priest of the witches, and the boundary lines are reputed to retain the 'power' raised by the witches. Symbolic cardinal points of the witch circle are: Boreas at the north, Zephyrus at the west, Notus at the south, and Eurus at the east.

Here are some circles and pentacles incorporating squares and triangles. It should be noted that though, strictly, a pentacle is a five-pointed star shape, witches use any circular object as a pentacle in their ceremonials.

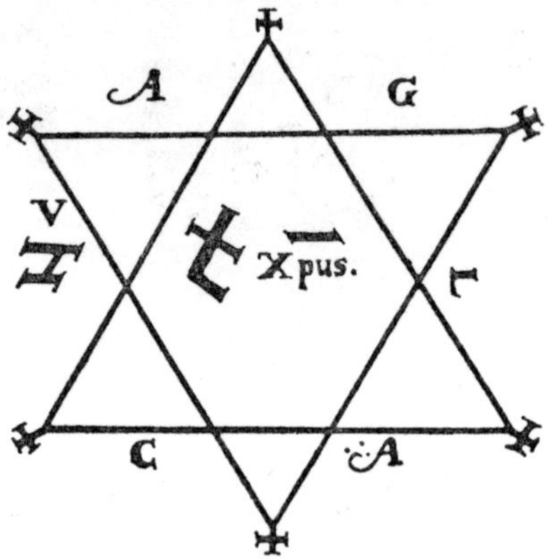

To make garments auspicious

Gypsy circle

To attract the good spirits

Triangle against fever

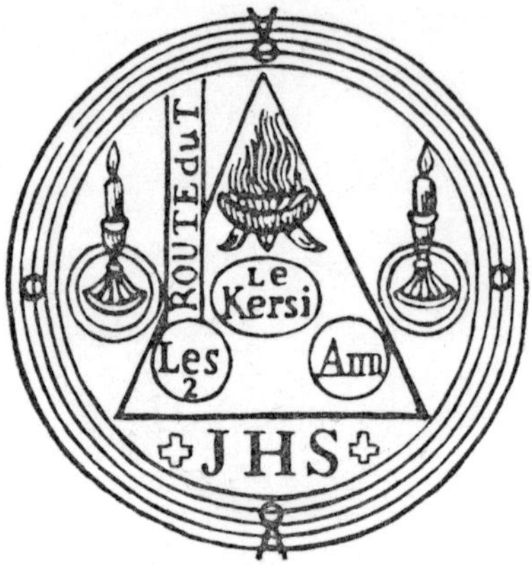

Circle of Pacts

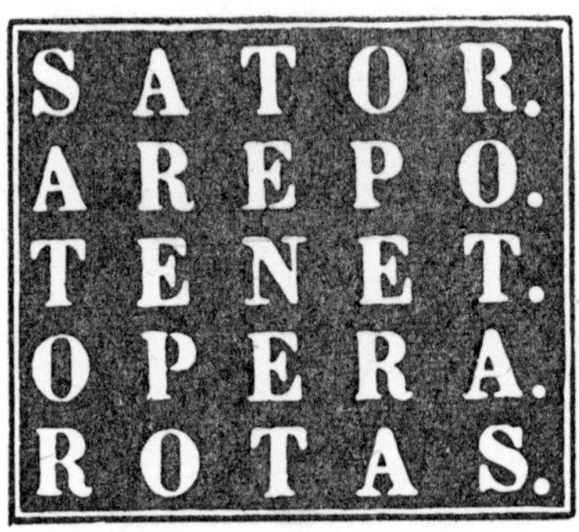

Square against conflagration

Occult number diagram of man

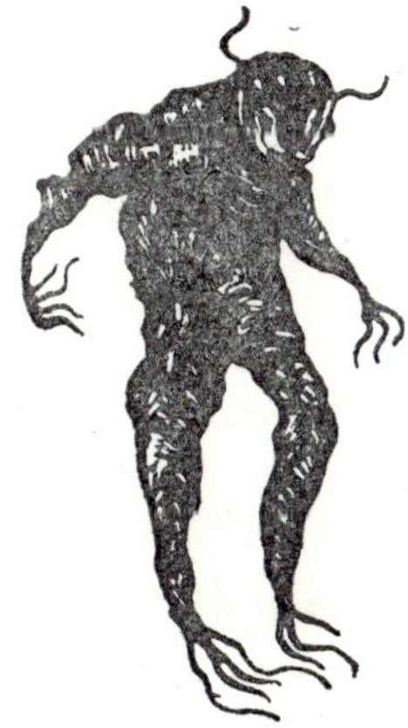

Mandrake—invulnerability

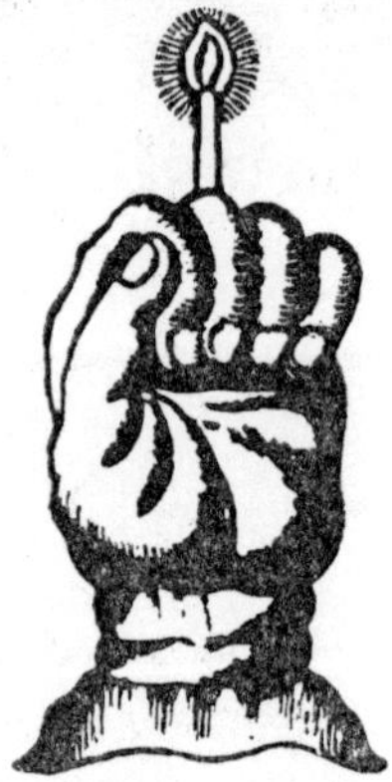

Hand of Glory—invisibility

Some African Symbols of Witchcraft

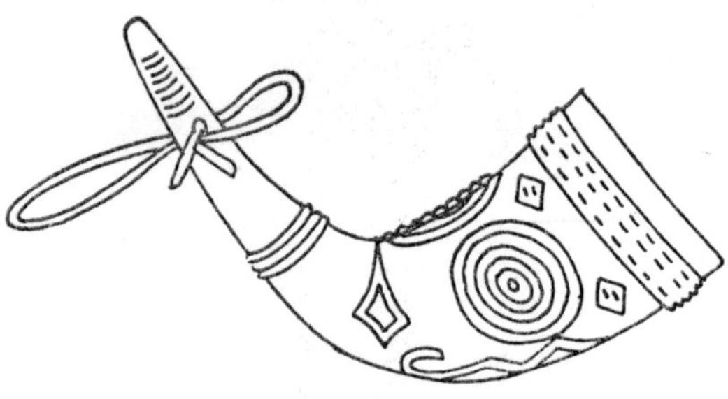

The symbolic Horn of the Kuba (Congo) tribe used in divination

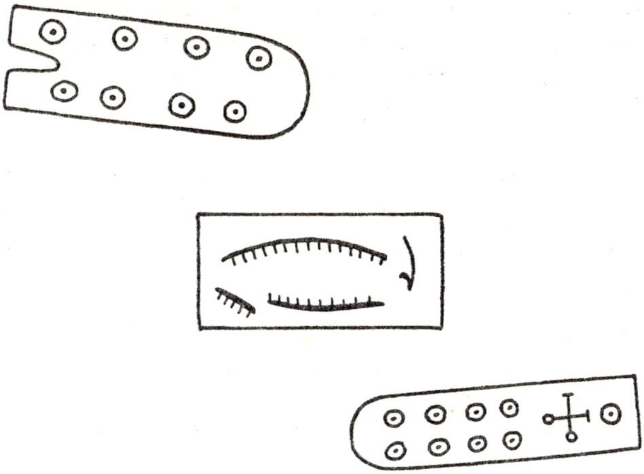

Markings on throwing stones

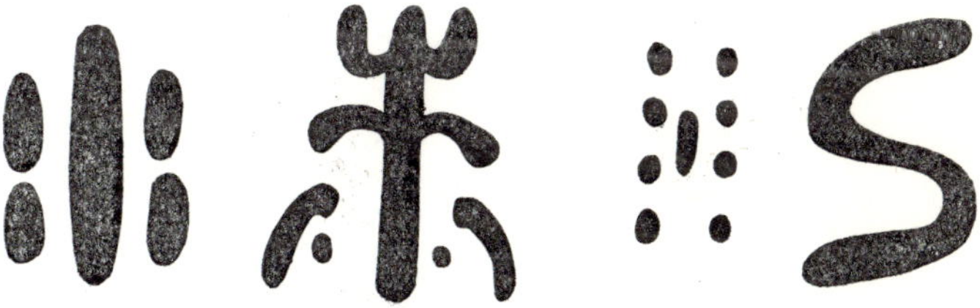

Symbols representing the spirits of animals and snakes

Divination

By legal definition, the crime which witches committed when using their powers of divination was one of deception, the law taking no account of the evil nature of the means employed. Thus when diviners were prosecuted their punishment was usually light; for instance in 1467, when one William Byg, an Englishman, was convicted of using a crystal stone to locate stolen property, his punishment was to appear in public with a label round his neck bearing the words *Ecce sortilegus* (Behold the fortune-teller).

In his *Mysmantia, the Mag-astro-mancer* (London, 1652), John Gaule set out the following list of the various methods of divination, seen here with some of the symbols of the individual arts:

Aeromancy, or divining by the air
Alectryomancy, by cocks or poultry
Alphitomancy, by meal, flour, or bran
Antinopomancy, by the entrails of women and children
Arithmancy, by numbers
Astragalomancy, by dice
Axinomancy, by saws
Botanomancy, by herbs
Capnomancy, by smoke

Aeromancy

Capnomancy

Carromancy, by melting of wax
Catoxtromancy, by looking-glasses
Cattabomancy, by vessels of brass or other metal
Cephalonomancy, by broiling of an ass's head
Chartomancy, by writing on papers

Chiromancy, by the hands
Chrystallomancy, by glasses
Cleromancy, by drawing lots
Coscinomancy, by sieves
Crithomancy, by grain or corn
Dactylomancy, by rings
Demonomancy, by the suggestion of evil demons
Gastromancy, by sounds from or signs on the belly

Gastromancy

Geomancy, by earth
Gyromancy, by rounds or circles
Hydromancy, by water
Icthyomancy, by fishes
Idolomancy, by the use of dolls, or images
Lampadomancy, by candles and lamps
Lecanomancy, by a basin of water
Lithomancy, by stones
Livanomancy, by the burning of frankincense
Logarithmancy, by logarithms
Macharomancy, by knives or swords
Oinomancy, by wine
Omphilomancy, by the navel
Oniromancy, by dreams

Geomancy

Lampadomancy

Necromancy

Onomatomancy, by names
Onychomancy, by the nails
Ornithomancy, by birds

Ornithomancy, or Augury if serpents were also used

Podomancy, by the feet
Psychomancy, by men's souls . . . or moral dispositions
Pyromancy, by fires
Roadomancy, by stars
Sciomancy, by shadows
Spatalamancy, by skins, bones and excrements
Stareomancy, or divining by the elements
Sternomancy, from the breast to the belly

Pyromancy

Roadomancy

Sycomancy, by figs
Theomancy, the pretence to divine by spirit revelation
Theriomancy, by beasts
Tuphramancy, by ashes
Tyromancy, by the coagulation of cheese

And in one word for all nagomancy or necromancy—by inspecting, consulting and divining by, with, or from the dead. A classic instance of necromancy is that of the Woman of Endor who was consulted by Saul (1 Samuel xxviii) when he wished to destroy the Philistine army. The woman, a medium, brought Samuel back from the dead to give advice.

Of all forms of divination this one of necromancy has fascinated man's mind most. Over and above his rites for hunting, fishing, fertility and self-preservation, it is the theme of death which, in all cultures, has dominated man's religion as much as magic. To appease the spirits of the dead, to ensure them a peaceful afterlife, to protect one's self from them, to propitiate them—these were the prime concerns of primitive man and the legacy to which latter-day witches fell heir.

For the most part, modern witches seem to have eschewed necromancy (except for one or two sporadic outbreaks of grave-robbing which have had more to do with Satanism than witchcraft), though it still remains an important part of certain Voodoo practices, as in Haiti. There, members of the Haitian *culte des mortes* (Creole for 'cult of the dead') use wooden crosses to call up Baron Samedi—'a tall black man with a long white beard and eyeless sockets in his head'—the spirit of graveyards and master of zombies. Each cross is dressed in a tail-coat and top-hat, and three lighted white wax candles are placed at the foot of the cross. Some propitiate Papa Legba, the guardian of death and the unknown.

In a full-scale practice of Haitian necromancy one person is chosen as the incarnation of Papa Nebo, father of death, and with two assistants, heads the procession to an isolated graveyard. After dressing a wooden cross as Baron Samedi, they kneel before it and knock two stones together to waken the Baron from sleep. Promises of gifts of food, drink and money are made and then, to close the consultation, a quantity of acacia leaves, balsam, roots and herbs are tossed towards the cross with the Creole words, *Dormi pa'fume, Baron Samedi*—'sleep sweetly, Baron Samedi'. A few minutes are allowed for the Baron to return to his slumbers, and then a corpse is disinterred from the graveyard. As with medieval witchcraft, the diviner representing Papa Nebo may now ask questions of the corpse.

At one time a flourishing group of necromancers practised divination in the Massif de la Hotte area of Haiti, south of Jérémie. Here people would gather from miles around, and like the European medium, one of their number would fall into a trance and, with a voice claimed to be that of a dead person, give advice or purport to deliver messages from the dead. If the medium was 'powerful' enough, faith-healing might be practised, although normally this was the prerogative of the *mamaloi* and *paprloi*, the male and female white witches of the orthodox Rada sect.

In 1929, when the famous American occultist and anthropologist, William Seabrook, was investigating Voodoo at first hand (see *The Magic Island*, 1929) necromancy was a powerful cult, and he quotes the case of one General Benoit Batraville, a revolutionary commander engaged in battle with the US occupation troops in 1920.

Batraville, it appears, turned to necromancy to divine the results of his war tactics, using a mixture of medieval witchcraft and Voodoo. Instead of the Creole incantations, he used such Latin phrases as *Exurgent mortui et acmo venuient*—'I require of you dead that you come to me'—coupled with the name of Astaroth, a figure of medieval European demonology. The spirit summoned, the general asked his questions, then laid it again by throwing a handful of graveyard dust 'to the four corners of the earth' saying, 'Go back from whence you came. From the dirt you were created, to the dirt you may return.'

England's most famous necromancer was, perhaps, the mathematician Dr John Dee (1527–1608), who became astrologer to Queen Elizabeth I, and is referred to in some manuscripts as 'Queen Elizabeth's Merlin'. His reputation as a magician has since obscured his undoubted brilliance as a mathematician, nor was it helped by his known association with a charlatan called Kelly. Dee is said 'to have evoked in 1582 as many famous dead people as he wanted to', a feat which many nineteenth-century mountebanks tried to emulate at public assemblies, some using the instructions laid down in the book *De mirabilius naturae, 1730*:

> Communication with the other world is easy . . . all that is needed is a bell made from an alloy of lead, tin, iron, copper, quicksilver, silver and gold. Write on it 'Adonai, Jesus, Tetrogrammaton'; and then for seven days place it in the middle of a ditch in a cemetery.

The Sorcery of Ancient Egypt

Early in their history the priests of On, at the city later to be called Heliopolis by the Greeks, evolved a cosmogony which showed how Rē-Atum, the great sun god, had generated himself out of Nun, the primordial ocean. Rē-Atum's offspring were Shu, the god of the air, and Tefnut, goddess of moisture, who in turn had given birth to Geb, the earth god, and Nut, the sky goddess, from whom sprung the deities Osiris, Isis, Set and Nephthys.

Set and Osiris became the two leading deities in Egyptian witchcraft, the former for black (evil) witch practices and the latter for white (good). As ruler of the netherworld, Osiris was always portrayed as a dead man, but he was also the great life-giver of Ancient Egypt and such was his acclaim and so popular did his cult become that he aroused the jealousy of his brother

Set (called by some Seth). Set eventually murdered Osiris, mutilated his body and scattered the pieces over Egypt.

After a while, Osiris was resurrected through the perseverance of his sister-wife Isis, who roamed the deserts in search of the dismembered limbs until she had collected them all. Horus, the son of Isis and Osiris, later avenged his father's murder by vanquishing Set and winning from him the rule of the earth.

Here an Ancient Egyptian witch petitions the *Ka* of a dead Pharaoh, who wears the Red Crown of Lower Egypt, for power in prognostication. The witch wears the panther skin which has always had a magical significance, as much in India and Africa as in Egypt. Its use is based on the belief that the strength of the panther will be vested in the wearer, but it also signifies ease of entry into the spirit world.

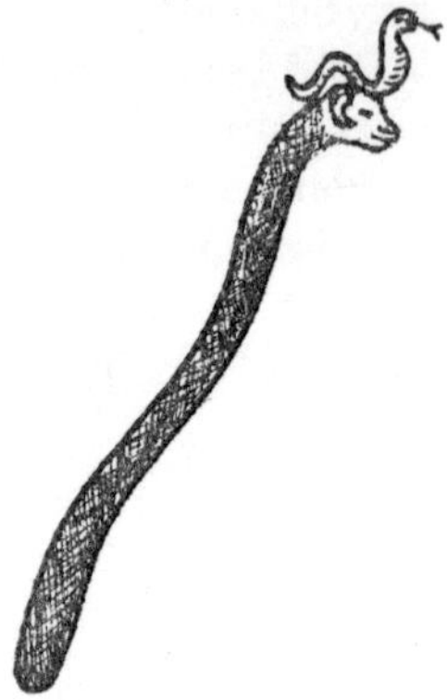

An Ancient Egyptian witch's wand, or magic stick. The horned head of the goat of Set surmounted by the uraeus symbolised the power to release nature's creative energies

In Ancient Egypt witches could summon the spirit of a dead king, or god, in order to petition favours simply by uttering the king's name, though worshippers of Set and Osiris (as with most of the nine chief deities of Egypt—the Great Ennead of Heliopolis) also had the mystic symbols of their cults carved on their house walls, or painted and traced with jewels on their clothes or body ornaments. In the case of Osiris, the *Akh* or *Khu*, symbolic of the rising sun of Osiris, was a popular personal emblem for mystic divination, while horns, or a goat figure, were the emblem of Set. All the witch had to do to work magic was to confront the symbol and utter the god's name.

In interesting contrast to the horned symbol of Set is the famous ram of the European witches.

Symbolic Curses

Perhaps the most famous curse of all time was that of Pharaoh Tutankhamun. His tomb in the Valley of the Kings, in Egypt, was reputed to be guarded by powerful supernatural forces and

The horned symbol of the Setian witches

The witches' ram symbol

it was said that certain death would be visited upon whosoever desecrated or opened the tomb.

In November 1922 his tomb was discovered by excavators and, thanks to the skill and patience of archaeologist and Egyptologist Howard Carter, the whole excavation was magnificently done so that a vast collection of Ancient Egyptian relics was saved for posterity.

No sooner had the excavation begun than fears were being voiced as to the retribution the *Ka* (spirit) of the dead Pharaoh would inflict upon those who had broken the seals of his tomb and, strangely enough, from February 1923 the excavators did begin to be plagued with problems quite unconnected with the archaeological work. Heated discussions leading to a quarrel between Howard Carter and Lord Carnarvon, who had the concession to undertake the dig, were claimed by the superstitious to be directly attributable to the mystic power of Tutankhamun. Of the incident, Professor Breasted writes:

> Bitter words were exchanged and in anger Carter requested his old friend to leave his house and never to enter

it again. Soon after this Lord Carnarvon fell ill with fever brought on by an infected wound. For some time he had been in poor health. Pneumonia set in, and on 5th April, 1923, at the age of 57, he died. The press attributed his death to an ancient curse, and sensationalised the superstition until it became a legend.

No further incidents appear to have been attributed to the curse, but there are many who will always believe in its potency and that it was fulfilled in the death of the unfortunate peer.

In all societies where witchcraft has been prevalent the most powerful weapon wielded by witches has always been thought to be the curse; and until comparatively recent times it was still possible to buy curses from those who had the 'power'. In the days of Roman Britain, the 'witches' did a good trade in selling small plates of metal with curses written upon them. A good example is the 'London Curse' found on a site in Prince's Street in London. Inscribed on a piece of lead which was once probably nailed to a door, the curse reads:

T(ITVS) EGNATIVS TYRANVS DEFIC(T)VS EST
ET P(VBLIVS) CICEREIVS FELIX DEFICTVS
E(S)T

Titus Egnatius Tyranus is hereby solemnly cursed;
likewise Publius Cicereius Felix

Thus for a few small coins, witches could help the little man who felt the forces of society were too powerful for him to combat alone.

Skull and Crossbones

Popular legend has it that the skull and crossbones emblem, once as common off the coasts of Florida and Georgia as it was in North Atlantic waters, was exclusively the trade-mark of pirates. In fact, pirates did not adopt the device until the seventeenth century, and there is evidence not only that the symbol was used much earlier but also that it had some association with witchcraft.

The carved device of skull and crossbones is often found in old cemeteries, particularly relating to eighteenth-century burials, but much earlier instances have been discovered of *real* skulls and crossbones, and there have been indications in some cases of their use in some form of mystic ritual.

When Professor Varley of University College, Accra, was excavating a site at Lissett, in the East Riding of Yorkshire, England, prior to the construction of an airfield in 1940, he came across a number of skull and crossbones burials; others have been found at Rushen Abbey, Isle of Man, and in Ireland. One of the Isle of Man burials revealed a strong clue to witchcraft practices, for one severed skull and thigh bones crossed at the chin was accompanied by a bronze figure of the Egyptian god Osiris; British Museum experts dated the burial as being of early or pre-Roman date.

Was this a case of the Egyptian god, with ceremonial knife and scourge, being used as a substitute high-priest figure in witchcraft? It seems likely, for Gerald B. Gardner records that 'in old times witches used a skull and crossbones to represent their god when his representative, the high-priest, was not present'.

The skull and crossbones have also been used from time to time as masonic emblems.

4

Witchcraft in North America

The first execution for witchcraft in the United States was that of Achsah Young of Massachusetts, who was hanged as a witch in May 1674. Long before that, however, a form of witchcraft had been practised by the Indian tribes, although in many cases on a very primitive level. Crude trickery is perhaps the best description of most accounts of Indian witchcraft given by early explorers, though it does on occasion appear to have prompted some useful remedial practices.

The medicine men of the Cherokees, for instance, knew how to amputate and cauterise, understood the principle of the tourniquet and, like their European brethren, were able to use herbs for medication and understood a curiously advanced form of hypnotism and auto-suggestion. There was also, of course, what might be called 'fringe' witchcraft, as for example the famous Mandan Rain Dance, which never failed eventually to produce rain simply because of the constant repetition of the ceremony.

A book, *Navaho Witchcraft* (Cambridge, Massachusetts, 1944), by C. Kluckhohn, gives a fascinating account, in the form of statements by informants, of early North American native witchcraft. It records that Navaho Indians believed (as did their African, Roman and medieval European counterparts) that witches could turn themselves into animals; that they gathered in cliques to feast off corpses, and exercised their powers by means of necrophily. The Navaho also seem to have shared with the Tiv tribe of Nigeria the belief that witches made use of the carcases of their victims as habitations and to enhance their mystical powers.

Kluckhohn mentions categories of persons held by the Navaho to be witch potential, and puts forward the novel idea that as the Navaho had few means of expressing aggression, without a belief in witchcraft they would have become a tribe of neurotics. As it was, their witchcraft, together with all other aspects of Indian culture in North America, was exterminated in the course of some two hundred years of wholesale slaughter.

So far as modern historians have been able to establish, only thirty-six people in all are known to have been executed for witchcraft in North America, and witch trials were nearly all confined to the northern English settlements in New England. Here the population were indeed 'people of God'. They had fled from England, practically denuding towns of the Midlands, because their consciences would not allow them to comply with the resurgence of royal authority in matters of religion, which had come with the English Restoration. And so on the rock-bound coast of Massachusetts they had founded a theocracy, where the elders of the chapels made and administered the laws according to their narrow view of the Bible.

In the minds of many of the Pilgrim Fathers, assiduous witch-hunters all, their new homes were in lands occupied by no less a power than the Devil himself. To these pious folk, the Indian inhabitants were demons personified who could summon attendant spirits and devils at will. As for the activities of the Indian shamans and the ability of these magicians to walk naked through fire and stab themselves painlessly with knives, this was the work of the Devil himself.

Within the area now entirely obliterated by the boundaries of the modern city of Ottawa lived a tribe of Indians who made up the original Algonquins ('fish-spearers'), an ethnic branch of a larger group of Indians who inhabited more southerly regions and who spoke the Algonquin set of languages. Ranging down the eastern seaboard of North America and the more inland eastern prairies, these were the Indians whom the first European colonists encountered in the sixteenth century. Pocahontas, the famous Indian princess of song, who married John Rolfe, an English settler, and who interceded with her father, chief Powhattan, for the life of Captain James Smith, the founder of Jamestown, was an Algonquin, and it was the Algonquins who inspired the *Brer Rabbit* stories of Joel Chandler Harris (1848–1908) and the magnificent *Hiawatha* of Henry Wadsworth Longfellow (1807–82).

Many Algonquin customs seem like witchcraft—the cultivation of sacred plants for mystic medicines, young girls dancing naked in the fields and forest, the worship of fire—and each individual tribe had its resident shaman, or medicine man, who would certainly be called a witch in any other society. From childhood those who experienced visions, suffered epileptic fits, or were apt to spend long periods alone, were deemed to have witch potential and 'power' to communicate with the spirits.

Spirit communication was important to all primitive tribes and the Algonquin Indians had their own special communicator, a shaman who mimed the flight of the mythical bird which, according to Indian legend, arose from the waters of the earth before the land was made by the Great Manitou, and brought back messages to the people—an interesting parallel to the Biblical story of Noah. For this ritual the shaman wore a bird head-dress, an otter pelt at his groin and a pouch of charms at his belt.

As in other forms of witch belief, the circle figured prominently in Algonquin rituals to 'raise the power'. A circle of small totem-poles (around 6ft in height), with grotesque figure-heads, was a permanent feature of each village and round the outer edge of the circle the shaman and his acolytes would dance in witch drama. It was believed that the power thus summoned helped the people to enjoy the fruits of the earth and protected them from evil. Among most North American Indians the medicine-man was credited with the ability to inflict sickness as well as to cure it and there is record of one occasion when a Papago tribe lynched a medicine-man for maliciously killing people with spells.

While greatly feared by many, a spirit often petitioned by the shamans was Chibiabos (Chipiapoos), Protector of the Land of the Dead. He is the singer of *Hiawatha*, and of him Longfellow wrote:

Most beloved by Hiawatha
Was the gentle Chibiabos,
He the best of all musicians,
He the sweetest of all singers.
Beautiful and childlike was he,
Brave as man is, soft as woman,
Pliant as a wand of willow,
Stately as a deer with antlers . . .
All the many sounds of nature
Borrowed sweetness from his singing;
All the hearts of men were softened
By the pathos of his music;
For he sang of peace and freedom,
Sang of beauty, love and longing;
Sang of death, and life undying
In the Islands of the Blessed,
In the kingdom of Ponemah
In the land of the hereafter.

Of all the witch-hunts in American history, perhaps none has been more widely publicised than those which took place at Salem (now Danvers), Massachusetts, in the year 1692. At that time tension was growing in New England, the colonies' constitution needed political clarification, both French soldiers and Indian warriors were waging guerrilla warfare, the winter had been cruel, smallpox raged, taxes were high, pirates were disrupting commerce and internecine land quarrels set neighbour against neighbour. As men and women became troubled in their own minds about the future for themselves and their families, their unquestioned belief in the supernatural took on a more sinister aspect and strengthened their belief that Satan himself was conspiring with certain evil mortals 'to threaten the subversion of the government', as Englishman John Evelyn was to record in his diary for 4 February 1693.

In the light of modern knowledge of psychology and the effects of mass emotion it has been possible to present a truer picture of the Salem Witches than the popular commentaries of the eighteenth and nineteenth centuries. And, quite contrary to the common assumptions then made about the Salem Witches, the following facts may be asserted.

The behaviour of the 'bewitched' persons was not fraudulent but a pathological affliction brought on, perhaps, by an obsessive interest in the occult. We know from the testimony of, for instance, the Rev Samuel Parris (a minister in Salem Village) that there was a time lag between the symptoms and the accusations: he records, 'When these calamities first began, which was in my own family, the affliction was several weeks before such hellish operations as witchcraft were suspected,' which would suggest that religious and medical practitioners in the village were perplexed by the symptoms, could not relate them to any known disease and blindly accepted the diagnosis of one of their number (tradition has it that it was Dr William Griggs of Salem Village) that, 'the evil hand' of malefic witchcraft was upon them.

That the people of Salem reached a state of excitement amounting almost to frenzy in their hunt for witches is true, but this was due more to superstition than to any preachings of the clergy. Likewise it can be said that Cotton Mather (1662–1728), Minister of God and Doctor of Theology in Harvard College, Massachusetts Bay Colony, son of the Rev Increase Mather (1639–1723), who was to be early America's most prolific writer on the supernatural, was by no means the anti-witch fanatic of tradition; if anything, he was a model of restraint and caution. In truth, we have noted that accusations of witchcraft were almost endemic among the common folk of the time, and the allegation that at Salem these were the result of pressure on the public by a corrupt leadership is just not true. What made the trials at Salem possible was a combination of circumstances which persuaded the community leaders (particularly the clergy) that there was some substance behind the accusations. The facts as now known, however, show that the clergy's part in the affair was far less culpable than has been alleged, that their restraint on the proceedings probably saved some lives, and certainly that their misgivings about the whole witch hunt finally brought the trials to an end.

To sum up the six main traditional delusions about the witch trials at Salem which are now discredited:

1. *That no witchcraft was practised at Massachusetts.* We need quote only one example (from the witchcraft case of Bridget Bishop) to prove that some did practise witchcraft at Salem. Two witnesses testified that Bridget Bishop hid in the cellar 'of the old house she formerly lived in . . . in holes in the old wall belonging to the said cellar . . . several puppets made up of rags and hogs' bristles with headless pins in them with the points outward. . . .'

2. *That the behaviour of the afflicted was fraudulent, designed only to call attention to themselves.* The afflicted were, in fact, mentally ill and had been for some time; they were hysterics in the clinical sense of the word.

3. *That the afflicted were coached by the clergy so that the latter might increase their personal hold over the community.* There is no evidence of this.

4. *That the clergy whipped the villagers into a state of mass hysteria.* Again unproven, superstition was no less strong than Bible lore.

5. *That the merchant class alone provided the opposition to the trials, particularly Thomas Brattle and Robert Calef.* As will be seen, the clergy were, in fact, the chief opponents of the trials. Again the writings of Brattle (*Letter of Thomas Brattle*) and Robert Calef (*More Wonders of the Invisible World*) came too late to influence the trials.

6. *That the executions were unique.* Obviously untrue.

After the Salem trials accusations of witchcraft ceased and in January 1697, five years after the trials, the jurors who had brought in the verdicts of guilty made their amends, and there was a community day of fasting in repentance for all the wrong-doings of the trials. As George Lincoln Burr was later to comment in his *The Literature of Witchcraft* (Papers of the American Historical Association, Vol IV, 1890): 'The New England panic at Salem was but a last bright flicker of the ghastly glare which had so long made hideous the European night.'

In 1957 the Commonwealth of Massachusetts finally reversed the attainders of all families accused of witchcraft and not covered by the eighteenth-century Acts.

Of one victim of the trials, Rebecca Nurse, hanged in July 1692, the poet John Greenleaf Whittier (1807–92) wrote in memory:

> O Christian martyr, who for Truth could die
> When all about thee owned the hideous lie,
> The world redeemed from Superstition's sway
> Is breathing freer for thy sake today.

Perhaps because they had been populated by more tolerant, and less credulous Episcopalians, the southern colonies of

America were far less affected by witch fanaticism. Few trials of witches are on record and cases like that of Grace Sherwood, tried and released in 1706 at Princess Anne County, Virginia, and the Rebecca Fowler hanging for witchcraft in Maryland 1685, were exceptional. Similarly, in South Carolina, few people were punished for witchcraft alone, but here there appears to have been an *acceptance* of witchcraft as an entity as, for example, in this instruction which Judge Nicholas Trott of Charleston gave to a jury in 1703:

> But this I think I may very well assert, that they that have given us good proof of apparitions and witches have done service to the common cause of religion, for if there be such creatures as witches, then there are certainly spirits by whose aid and assistance they act, and by consequence there is another invisible world of spirits. . . . Yet that there are creatures as witches I make no doubt, neither do I think that they can be denied, without denying the truth of the Holy Scriptures, or most grossly perverting the sense of them.

From 1648 to 1691, apart from Salem, little more than a dozen witches were executed in New England, a few others being condemned to banishment or whipping. In fact, it might be said that the history of North American witchcraft is largely Salem, for New York was virtually free from the witchcraft delusion; Rhode Island had a law against witchcraft but held no trials; Connecticut executed only four alleged witches; Pennsylvania was without statutes against witches until 1717; and in New Hampshire one Jane Welford was charged at Dover in 1656 but subsequently released to be of good behaviour.

An interesting sidelight on witchcraft in North America, and in some respects unique, was the fact that a number of those accused of witchcraft were able to sue their detractors for slander—and some won their cases.

In Central and South America, witchcraft may perhaps be

said to have reached its zenith in the days of the Aztecs. In their great capital at Tenochtitlan, set near the huge pyramid dedicated to the War God, a college of witches, soothsayers and magicians was maintained, not unlike the ancient Roman college of Augurs, where priests were trained to interpret signs of divine approval from the movement, flight and song of birds, for instance, or even from accidental occurrences. Here all manner of courses in the black arts were taught in a branch of the Calmecac, the Aztecs' priestly university. Inevitably, the invading Spaniards saw the whole Aztec religion as Devil-inspired witchcraft, and the Conquistadores burned their ancient books and destroyed their temples as artefacts of the Devil. Thus was native witchcraft ruthlessly stamped out in Central and South America, the Inquisition being imported for the purpose. Significantly, there survives one form of witchcraft called Nagualism, which is specifically directed against the white invaders. This grew up among Indians following the Spanish invasion and is still practised today in the remote jungles of Central America.

From the seventeenth century onwards, only isolated cases of witch practice are recorded in North American country journals and would often appear to coincide with times of local trouble when the discovery of a witch would provide a convenient scapegoat for the community. With the coming of the twentieth century, witchcraft cases begin to occur with greater frequency, again mostly coinciding with times of national crisis. Thus the years from World War I to the 'depression' and those leading up to World War II were particularly well marked by accusations of witchcraft. Here are a few examples:

10 April 1931. In Wilkes-Barre, twenty-nine-year-old Mrs Carl Thomsen killed Miss Minnie Dilley, aged seventy-six, with a knife and a ginger-ale bottle. 'She has cast', alleged Mrs Thomsen, 'a spell over me and my husband, and it was her life or mine.' The practice of attacking witches with bottles is curiously American.

2 October 1936. At Woodbridge, New Jersey, Mrs Terese Czinkota was accused by three women neighbours of being a witch. The charge against her was heard in a magistrate's court where Mrs Czinkota was accused of making 'her body change into an animal's', the complainants testifying as to 'certain brews and potions' made by the accused for evil purposes. The Recorder, Arthur Brown, threw the case out of court.

29 July 1939. Newark, New Jersey. The *Ledger* reports a case in which a negro, John Baptistalk, was accused of witchcraft and was held on bail under grand jury indictment. He had been giving credulous people 'magical baths' and had kept one assistant busy visiting a cemetery at midnight to bring back earth from a freshly-dug grave.

1 January 1940. Mora, New Mexico. Evelion Espinosa was accused of 'turning himself into a frog' and casting spells on his neighbours. Testimony was given to the effect that Espinosa 'acted queerly on Christmas night and made signs on the floor' near the beds of his wife and his cousin, after which he had mutilated them. Assistant District Attorney R. E. Cooper said that the mountain folk had long accused Espinosa of being 'the man who turns into a frog'.

A comment on the contemporaneous witch scene in North America will be found in Chapter 10.

5

Sabbats, Feasts and Festivals

The concept of the witch festival is of ancient origin, and as early as the ninth century the idea was current that witches rode 'at night with Diana on certain beasts'. Whether or not the early witches did actually foregather in a common ritual, much as those practising witchcraft deviations today do at certain times of the year, is debatable but certainly from ancient times the witches' calendar has been marked by eight great celebrations. These were February Eve, or Candlemas (1 February), the Spring Equinox (20 March), May Eve (30 April), the Summer Solstice, or Midsummer Night Festival (21 June), August Eve or Lammas (31 July), the Autumn Equinox (20 September), Hallowe'en (31 October) and the Festival of Rebirth (20 December). The February, May, August and October ceremonies may have had some connection with the Ancient Gaelic year and correspond to festivals for Bealteine, or Beltane, Lugnasadh, Samhaim, or Samhuin, and Brigid, the goddess of home crafts and hearths. Thus the witches' original calendar bears a close resemblance to the pagan cycle of seeding, harvesting and animal procreation.

From 1484 onwards, from the records of witch persecution in Europe, we can form some idea of the two main types of meetings that took place: a periodic *esbat*, which all the local witches attended, and a *sabbat*, usually held four or eight times a year, to which witches came from miles around. Though often misnamed the 'Witches' Sabbath', the sabbat had no Christian connotation and the word is more likely to have derived from the French *esbattre*, to frolic, or from the name of the Thracian god of beer, Sabazius. The Christian Sabbath derives from the Jewish Shabat, from *sheba* (seven), and the witches did not have associations in seven day cycles.

Pagan and early assemblies apart, the conception of the sabbat as something evil in itself seems to have been fostered, if not invented, by the Inquisition during the fourteenth and fifteenth centuries, entirely for their own ends. In other words, the Inquisition, by establishing that witches *did* meet as a group at set times to parody the Christian liturgy, planned to incite hostility against them through fear that they might thus work magic to the detriment of the local community.

In time, sabbats were deemed to have a five-part ceremonial:

1. *The Convocation.* Though there has been much controversy as to the particular day of the weeks on which sabbats were usually held, it now appears that witches gathered whenever they pleased, but always at night. They were reputed to reach the assembly point by various means of transvection using potions for travel, or riding on forked sticks or brooms, and the sabbat lasted until dawn, or cockcrow.

According to Reginald Scot, who wrote *Discoverie of Witchcraft* (London, 1584), witches met in certain places:

> As for the places of Magical Circles, they are to be chosen melancholy, doleful, dark and lonely; either in Woods or

> Deserts, or amongst ruins of Castles, Abbeys, Monasteries, &c, or upon the Seashore when the Moon shines clear, or else in some large Parlour hung with black and the floors covered with the same, with doors and windows closely shut, and waxen candles lighted.

But in practice witches' meeting-places varied enormously. A crossroads or, better still, a meeting of three roads or paths, was a very popular site for a witches' meeting, a concourse of three ways being considered sacred to the Luna-Diana-Hecate triptych. And long after their association with witches had been all but forgotten, such places continued to be regarded by the local communities as unhallowed, fit sites for suicides to be buried and the corpses of miscreants hung in chains.

Very often witches' meetings took place beside running water, to which magic properties have always been attributed, or beside oak trees or yews, which were planted by the Druids as sacred groves in which to grow the magic mistletoe sacred to both Norse and Greek mythology. Any particularly great oak, sinister-looking tree, or queer-shaped boulder was consequently deemed the meeting-place of witches, as is seen in the many Devil's Oaks and Devil's Rocks which exist as commonly in Montana, Nebraska and Colorado, as they do in Dumfriesshire, Yorkshire and Northumberland.

In some European countries like Sweden, however, witches favoured specially built houses called *Blockula*, containing several rooms and a chapel, and set in an open field or wood.

2. *The Veneration.* All sabbats included some ritual of allegiance to Satan, whether there was to be a rebaptism by the high-priest, a witch 'marriage' or some other form of initiation. Describing a Continental sabbat in his *Compendium Maleficiarum* Francesco-Maria Guazzo notes:

> When (the witches) have met together, they generally light a foul and horrid fire. The Devil is president of the assembly and sits on a throne, in some terrible shape, as of

> a goat or a dog; and they approach him to adore him, but not always in the same manner. For sometimes they bend their knees as suppliants, and sometimes they stand with their backs turned, and sometimes they kick their legs high up so that their heads are bent back and their chins point to the sky. They turn their backs and, going backwards like crabs, put out their hands behind them to touch him in supplication. When they speak they turn their faces to the ground; they do all things in a manner altogether foreign to the use of other men. . . .

Next came the *osculum infame*, or *osculum obscoenum*, the famed 'kiss of shame'; of which Guazzo notes:

> Then they offer him pitch-black candles, or infants' navel cords; and kiss him upon the buttocks in sign of homage (*ad signum homagii eum in podicem osculantur*). Having committed these and similar execrable abominations, they proceed to other infamies.

3. *The Manducation.* An orgy of gluttony is the general picture of the sabbat, and again we may look to Guazzo for a classic account of sabbat feasting:

> There are tables placed and drawn up, and they sit and start to eat of the food which the demon has provided, or which they have themselves brought. But all who have sat down to such tables confess that the feasts are all foul either in appearance or in smell, so that they would easily nauseate the most hungry stomach. . . . They say that there is plenty of everything except bread and salt.

Writing around 1611, Sister Madeleine de Demandolx gives fuller details:

> The drink which they have is malmsey (a strong, sweet wine), to provoke and prepare the flesh to luxurious wantonness. . . . The meat they ordinarily eat is the flesh of

young children, which they cook and make ready in the synagogue (a common anti-Semitic reference of the sixteenth and seventeenth centuries), sometimes bringing them thither alive by stealing them from the houses where they have opportunity to come. They have no use of knives at table for fear lest they should be laid across (a superstition still common in country districts)... they have also no salt, which figureth out wisdom and understanding; neither know they the use of olives or oil which represent mercy.

4. *The Celebration.* Following the feast came the dances 'which are performed in a circle but always to the left...', music being provided by some of the other witches present, 'viols and other instruments, which are brought thither by those that were skilled to play upon them' (see Sebastian Michaëlis, *Histoire admirable de la possession et conversion d'une pénitente*, Paris, 1613).

5. *The Copulation.* The dancing over, the witches then 'gave themselves over to copulation . . .'. Writing in his *Tableau de l'inconstance des mauvais anges* (Description of the Inconstancy of Evil Angels, 1612), Pierre de Rosteguy, Sieur de Lancre, a trial judge in France, gave what he claimed to have been an eyewitness account of copulation with the Devil at a sabbat:

> The Devil in the form of a goat, having his member in the rear, had intercourse with women by joggling and shoving that thing against their belly. Marie de Marigrane, aged fifteen years, a resident of Biarritz, affirmed that she had often seen the Devil couple with a multitude of women, whom she knew by name and surname, and that it was the Devil's custom to have intercourse with the beautiful women from the front, and with the ugly from the rear.

The festival which is most associated in popular legend with witches is, of course, All Hallow's Eve, or Hallowe'en, once a festival of the dead and the powers of darkness, but now most often celebrated by children, especially in the United States.

In his famous book *The Golden Bough,* Sir James George Frazer (1854–1941) put Hallowe'en in historical perspective:

> . . . throughout Europe, Hallowe'en, the night which marks the transition from autumn to winter, seems to have been of old the time of year when the souls of the departed were supposed to revisit their old homes in order to warm themselves by the fire and to comfort themselves with the good cheer provided for them in the kitchen or the parlour by their affectionate kinsfolk. It was, perhaps, a natural thought that the approach of winter should drive the poor shivering hungry ghosts from the bare fields and the leafless woodlands to the shelter of the cottage with its familiar fireside. . . .

Thus bonfires on high hills were a conspicuous feature of old Hallowe'en rites, presumably as the people preferred to entertain the dead while in a crowd rather than in the solitude of their own homes. Originally, the bonfires were probably meant to provide heat and light for those at the rites and, mystically, to help the sun store up power for the cold winter months. Gradually the Hallowe'en bonfires were transferred in England to the 5 November and the celebration of the arrest of Guy Fawkes, who attempted to blow up the Houses of Parliament in 1605. Nevertheless, only a hundred years ago one traveller to Scotland counted some thirty hilltop fires on Hallowe'en between Dunkeld and Aberfeldy, each with its circle of dancers.

One prominent Hallowe'en ceremony, 'Leeting the Witches', was observed in Lancashire, where it was generally believed that witches met on this night at Malkin Tower, a ruined old farm in Pendle Forest, once the home of the supposed witch Elizabeth Southerns (alias Old Demdike). It was believed that if a lighted candle were carried about the neighbouring fells from 11 pm to midnight, and if it burned steadily during that hour, any witches gathering in the vicinity would be disconcerted; on the other hand if the candle were extinguished trouble would befall its carrier. Any witches in the area were believed to do everything in their power to extinguish the candle.

In many cases it was thought that fiery brands vigorously waved about would drive away witches. Sometimes this rhyme was chanted in Scotland, while firebrands were waved to discourage the assembly of witches at Hallowe'en:

> This is the nicht o' Hallowe'en,
> A' the witches are to be seen,
> Some o' them black, an' some o' them green,
> And some o' them like a randy queen.
> Hallowe'en we fear will come
> Witchcraft will be done by some
> Burn my brand and let us see
> Confusion to the witches be.

Once it was widely believed that demons and hobgoblins, witches who straddled broomsticks, and ghosts who rode on black headless horses, all appeared at Hallowe'en, and in Queen Victoria's time in Balmoral, Scotland, the effigy of a witch was burnt to keep away such powers of evil.

Today at Hallowe'en, particularly in the northern part of England, *guisers* go from door to door singing and dancing, dressed in curious home-made costumes and grotesque masks, the only remaining outward sign that they are taking part in an age-old mystic custom. Such costumes and masks, not forgetting the lighted turnip or pumpkin lanterns, are also common in the United States at this time, and children still visit neighbours for food-offerings, morsels which once belonged to the dead.

Modern witches still gather at Hallowe'en to ask the souls of the dead to manifest themselves or give messages.

Folk superstition tells of another day when the witches were supposed to be out in full force; this was Hansel Monday (the first Monday after New Year) and people did not get out of bed early that morning since the witches did not disperse until sunrise.

In centuries past, town and village folk alike went to great lengths to rid themselves of witches, forming night patrols, often headed by the local clergyman chanting Latin psalms, to discourage the assembly of witches. But the townsfolk of Dewsbury, in Yorkshire, went one step further, their target being the arch-witch, the Devil himself. On Christmas Eve, just as the first stroke of midnight was heard, the 'Devil's Knell' was rung from the belltower of Dewsbury parish church (a custom which still takes place every year). This custom of ringing the 'Devil's Knell' dates from the middle ages, when a local squire, Sir Thomas de Soothill, committed a murder. To expiate his crime, he donated a bell to the parish church and this became known as 'Black Tom of Soothill'.

Ringing the 'Devil's Knell' was revived in 1828, discontinued again during World War II, when bells were only tolled as a signal of German invasion, and revived again in 1945.

Formerly the tenor bell was raised and five-fives were rung first, in order to announce that the Devil had passed. Four-fours came next as man's knell, followed by three-threes for that of woman. The bell was then tolled for the birth of Christ.

In the old days, the people of Dewsbury strongly believed that the Devil and his entourage could be kept away from the town by tolling the parish church bell once for every year of the Christian Era, and few people rested easy in their beds until the last peal had died away.

At the end of June, the St John's Eve chain of bonfires was a regular occurrence in many centres in Cornwall, including St Ives, Penzance, Helston, Camborne, Redruth, Truro, St Austell, Liskeard and Callington. This custom is undoubtedly of pagan witchcraft origin, but was later adopted in honour of St John. Words in Cornish (incantations) are pronounced and a bunch of flowers (offerings) thrown into the flames. In some cases young couples jump through the flames to ensure married bliss.

The Festival of Rebirth (called by some 'the Cauldron of Regeneration, and 'the Dance of the Wheel') is still important to present-day witches for it symbolises the rebirth of the sun and the assured return of summer. Ritual varies, but usually a circle is cast and purified and cakes and wine are eaten by those present; then a cauldron is set in the middle of the circle and filled with spirit which is ignited. Facing each other the priestess and high-priest lead the chant while the others present begin to dance round the circle, holding torches high in a 'sunwise' direction, some jumping over the cauldron. When the flames have died away, the priestess completes the dance routine and the feast follows.

In this ceremony the chant is of great importance:

Queen of the Moon, Queen of the Sun,
Queen of the Heavens, Queen of the Stars,
Queen of the Waters, Queen of the Earth,
Bring to us the Child of Promise (ie, the Sun).

It is the great mother who giveth birth to him,
It is the Lord of Life who is born again.
Darkness and tears are set aside
When the Sun shall come up early.

Golden Sun of the Mountains,
Illumine the Land, Light up the World,
Illumine the Seas and the Rivers,
Sorrow be laid, Joy to the World.

Blessed be the Great Goddess,
Without beginning, without end,
Everlasting to eternity.
I.O.EVO.HE Blessed Be.

In several European countries, customs which had their origin in witchcraft ritual still survive: here are a representative few.

A curious carnival custom is perpetuated each year in the small Tyrolean towns of Imst, Thaur, Telfs and Nassereith, in

Austria. Those partaking in the ceremony, know as *Schemen-laufen*, wear horrific wooden masks (often prized heirlooms) and act out ancient rituals to drive away the winter witches.

All over Denmark, on 23 June, men and women take part in a national rejoicing for the longest day of the year. Along the coast, particularly north of Copenhagen, thousands of bonfires fling their sparks into the long twilight, while a witch effigy is burnt, a reminder of the once widespread belief that a witch effigy thus burnt increased the powers which gave sailors safety at sea.

One of the most famous of all witches' meeting-places was the summit of the spectacular Puy de Dôme, in the Auvergne mountains of Central France. Here in this agricultural area is the site of a temple of Mercury whose spirit the witches adopted for their own special pantheon.

In the Harz mountains of Germany they still celebrate *Walpurgis Nacht*, 30 April, when witches flying from Brocken, the highest mountain in northern Germany, are driven out in noisy pitched battles. It was once believed that those who participated and so aided the good spirits would be rewarded with good fortune and ample crops throughout the coming year. Braunlage, Toffaus and Bad Harzburg are the main centres of these Walpurgis Night festivities.

At Langades (and Ayi Eleni, reached from Salonica), Greece, there takes place on 21 May the Anastesaria Feast, celebrated in accordance with traditional pagan and Byzantine rites; this festival includes the spectacle of townspeople walking barefoot on burning embers, once a favourite trick of local witches in ages past.

Epiphany celebrations at Tarcento, Italy, comprise a group of interesting festivities which, according to ancient tradition, culminate in a torchlight procession to the top of a hill where once witches danced in mystic supplication round a fire. The volume of smoke exuding from the bonfire was held to be an augury of the degree of success which would attend the year's harvest.

6

Mystic Charms and Flying Ointments

Near the top of the shopping-lists of the women of Ancient Greece, some 2,000 years ago, would have come a variety of charms and potions for the relief of pain, enhancement of beauty and increased potency in love-making.

In his *Aus einem griechischen Zauberpapyrus* (Bonn 1911), R. Wunsch tells of one very potent concoction of the Greek witches, which, with the correct incantation, might be used for a variety of purposes:

> Take a shrewmouse and *idolise* (ie, drown) it in spring water; do the same with two moon-headed beetles, but in running water; then take a crawfish, fat from a speckled virgin goat, dung from the dog-headed ape, two ibis eggs, two *drachmae* (*drachma*—the basic silver coin of Ancient Greece, also a weight, literally one 'handful') each of gum,

myrtle resin and crocus; four *drachmae* each of Italian Alpine herb and incense and an onion without any sucker. Place all these things in a mortar, pound them carefully, and keep the mixture in case of necessity in a leaden receptacle. When you want to use it, take some and go to the loft with a coal-pan, and when the moon rises, offer the mixture with the following prayer, and Selene (goddess of the Moon) will immediately appear.

First, then, came the prayer to the goddess and then the petition:

For illness: 'Make ——, the son/daughter of ——, sick.'

For death: 'Take the breath, O beautiful Mistress, from the nose of ——.'

For a dream: 'Come to him/her in the form of the goddess, whom —— serves.'

For advice: 'Come to me, beloved goddess, and given me during sleep advice concerning ——.'

Four spells, in fact, for the price of one, but on the container the witch-manufacturer might write: 'Do not employ the charm too rashly, but only when you have serious reason for it.'

It was common enough in Ancient Greece for the girl who had lost her lover to consult a witch to win him back. In *Dialogues of the Courtesans*, Lucian leaves an interesting example of this belief:

> *Bacchis:* I know an old Beldam, by Nation a Syrian (to the Greeks, Syria was the land which exported witches and all manner of magic practices). When my Lover deserted me on a Pike of Jealousy, as yours now has done; after Four whole Months by her Art we were reconcil'd, when I despaired of seeing him, but compell'd by her Charms, he return'd into my Arms.
>
> *Melissa:* Well, do you remember what Reward you gave her?
>
> *Bacchis:* No great matter, half a Crown and Bread, and

you must mingle Seven Single Pennies with Salt, together with Incense and a Torch; she mingles a Bowl of Wine, and drinks it herself: There must be some Moveable of the Party's, as some of his Clothes, Slippers, Hair, or something which belong'd to him.

Melissa: I have his Slippers by me.

Bacchis: These being hung upon a Pole, and fum'd with Incense and sprinkling Salt on the Fire: After this, she pronounces the Names of you both. Then drawing a Wand out of her Bosom, which she turns every way, repeating the Incantation with a voluble Tongue, and Words of horrible sound. When she had perform'd this, he quarrell'd with his Comrades and Associates, and with Phebis his then Mistress, and return'd to me again. Besides, she instructed me in a Charm to preserve his Hatred of Phebis: That I should mind when he departed from me and should blot out his Footsteps with mine, and place my Right Foot on his Left, and the contrary on the Right, saying ON THEE I TREAD, AND AM THY HEAD. And I did as she commanded me.

Melissa: Make no delay, but call the Syrian quickly, and prepare all things necessary for the Conjuration.

In the early *Malleus Maleficarum*, the authors set out seven rules to distinguish a good charm from an evil one, in light of the fact that licit medicine was then often of a charm-herbal nature. A charm was allowable if it involved:

1. No suggestion in words of any pact with the Devil.
2. No unknown names.
3. Nothing untrue.
4. The only ritual the signing of the cross.
5. No credence in the *manner* of writing or reciting the charm, or of wearing or using it.
6. Only biblical phrases in their original context.
7. Assurances that the efficacy depended wholly on the will of God.

Thus mystic amulets and talismans were ruled out, or any object inscribed with magic letters or the Witches' Alphabet. Should disc-charms or labels be worn about the person they should only contain authorised biblical quotations.

Somewhere in her house, it was supposed, a witch would keep a chest or cabinet containing a bizarre collection of powders and potions. The many herbs to be found in a witch's kitchen will be mentioned in greater detail in Chapter 8 but for now we can examine the contents of the traditional *witch's stockpot.* In *Macbeth,* William Shakespeare left with us a picture of the customary witch's cauldron holding many witch-related items which readily spring to mind today:

Round about the cauldron go;
In the poison'd entrails throw.
Toad, that under cold stone
Days and nights has thirty-one
Swelter'd venom sleeping got,
Boil thou first i' the charmed pot . . .
Fillet of a fenny snake,
In the cauldron boil and bake;
Eye of newt, and toe of frog,
Wool of bat, and tongue of dog,
Adder's fork, and blind-worm's sting,
Lizard's leg, and owlet's wing . . .
Scale of dragon, tooth of wolf,
Witches' mummy, maw and gulf
Of the ravin'd salt-sea shark,
Root of hemlock digg'd i' the dark,
Liver of blaspheming Jew,
Gall of goat, and slips of yew
Sliver'd in the moon's eclipse,
Nose of Turk, and Tartar's lips,
Finger of birth-strangled babe
Ditch-deliver'd by a drab,

Make the gruel thick and slab:
Add thereunto a tiger's chaudron,
For the ingredients of our cauldron.

Little less bizarre were the witch objects found in a Bronze Age grave in Denmark, as noted by Arne Runeberg 'Witches, Demons and Fertility Magic' (*Commentiones humanarum litterarum*, Helsingfors, 1947, Vol 114, No 4):

The claw of a lynx (used as an amulet and as a medicine)
Bones of a weasel (used as a medicine for sick animals)
Vertebrae of snakes (used as above)
Horses' teeth (hung round children's necks to make teeth strong)
Rowan twig (for charms)
Charcoal of aspen (powerful magic powder)
Iron pyrites (used in ill-willing)

Among the special charm potions manufactured by witches were three important ointments; one for flying (transvection), one for changing into animals (metamorphosis) and one for killing.

Transvection

A universal feature of witchcraft has always been nocturnal flight through the air, and popular illustrations of witches depict the broomstick as the regular vehicle for flight, although cleft sticks, distaffs and shovels are also mentioned. According to the very early *Errores Gazariorum* (1450), a stick (*baculum*) was presented, together with a pot of 'flying ointment', to every new witch after she had rendered the Devil the kiss of shame.

The ointment was usually made—to quote the treatise on witchcraft by Sylvester Prierias, the Vatican's famous troubleshooter sent to champion the Faith against Luther (*De Strigimagarum Daemonumque Mirandis*, Rome, 1521)—'from a thick stew of boiled children, preferably unbaptised'. To which

Francis Bacon, in his *Sylva Sylvarum,* satirically added 'the fat of children digged out of their graves' when mixed with fine meal and 'the juices of smallage, wolfbane, and cinquefoil' proved by far the best ingredients for flying ointment, which was rubbed on the body until the skin glowed bright pink.

It is interesting to note that in several early European cultures there was a fertility rite to bring good crops which involved riding a pole or broom as a hobby-horse. No doubt the early witches practised this rite, and as they leaped high in the air would seem to observers to be flying.

The earliest pictures of witches in flight come from Ulrich Molitor's *De Lamiis et Phitonicis Mulieribus* (Concerning Female Sorcerers and Soothsayers) of 1489, a copy of which may be found in Cornell University Library, in the United States.

Metamorphosis

The belief that human beings could take the form of animals was once widespread and is still today the basis of the witchcraft practised by primitive African tribes, and especially of their secret societies. Traditionally, the transformation was brought about by the use of certain ointments and during the trial of the Salmesbury witches in Lancashire, in 1612, the recipe for such a salve was mentioned. Having dug up the corpse of a child:

> 'they (ie, the witches Jannet and Ellen Bierley) did boil some thereof in a pot, and some did boil on the coals. . . . And afterwards the said Janet and Ellen did seethe the bones of the said child in a pot, and with the fat that came out of the said bones, they said they would anoint themselves, that thereby they might sometimes change themselves into other shapes.

After rubbing their bodies with the ointment, some witches (see, particularly, the Scottish Witch Trial of Isobel Gowdie, 1662) uttered incantations:

When we go in the shape of a hare, we say thrice over:

I shall go into a hare,
With sorrow and sigh and mickle care;
And I shall go in the Devil's name
Ay while I come home again.

And instantly we start in a hare.
And when we would be out of this shape, we will say:

Hare, hare, God send thee care.
I am in a hare's likeness just now,
But I shall be in a woman's
Likeness even now.

Other common metamorphoses were, Lycanthropy (witch into wolf); Aeluranthropy (into cat); Boanthropy (into cow); Kuanthropy (into dog); and Lepanthropy (into hare).

The most typical transformations reported in England were of human into horse, pig, cat, dog and bear, as Shakespeare notes in *A Midsummer Night's Dream:*

Sometimes a horse I'll be, sometimes a hound,
A hog, a headless bear, sometimes a fire,
And neigh, and bark, and grunt, and roar and burn
Like horse, hound, dog, bear, fire, at every turn.

Killing Ointment

It was once commonly believed that poisoning people was among the *maleficia* of witches, to which end the third most important ointment was used.

Usually made from human bones, venomous snakes and reptiles, fats from animals and powdered dried fish, the lethal concoction could be administered for inhalation, oral consumption, or as an ointment.

Among other formulae for killing ointments, as recorded by Johan Weyer, physician to the Duke of Cleaves, was:

Hemlock, juice of aconite
With popular leaves and roots bind tight.
Mix water cress and oil
To baby's fat and boil.
Some bat's blood and belladonna too
Will kill off those who misuse you.

Another traditional piece of folklore tagged on to witchcraft was that witches could raise storms. In his *History of Travel in the West and East Indies* (1577), clearly copying Olaus Magnus *Historia de Gentibus Septentrionalibus* (1555), Richard Eden described how Finnish witches raised storms:

> They tie three knots on a string hanging at a whip. When they loose one of these, they raise tolerable winds. When they loose another, the wind is more vehement. But by loosing the third, they raise plain tempests, as in old time they were accustomed to raise thunder and lightning.

Some witches offered for sale potions and devices guaranteed to raise storms and winds, and as late as 1814 a woman called Bessie Millie of Stromness, on the mainland of Orkney, sold 'winds by the Devil's help to seamen'. Sir Walter Scott bought one of these charms and recorded the fact in his diary.

From *The Boke of the Mervayles of the World* we can take further examples of witch charms and spells:

Love charm

> If thou wilt that a woman bee not visious nor desire men, take the private members of a Woolfe, and the haires which doe grow on the cheekes or eyebrowes of him, and haires which bee under his beard, and burne it all, and give it to her to drinke, when she knoweth not, and she shal desire no other man.
>
> And it is said, when a woman desireth not her husband; then let him take a little of the tallow of a bucke Goat—

meane between little and great—let him anoint his privy members with it, and do the acte of generation. She shal love him, and shal no doe the act of generation afterwards with any other man.

'*Charm for the Improving of Memorie*'

If the heart, eye and brain of a Lapwing or black plover be hanged upon a man's necke, it is profitable against forgetfulness and sharpeneth man's understanding.

'*Ane Charm to See the Fairies*'

A pint of Sallet oyle and put it in a vial glasse; and first wash it with rose water; the flowers to be gathered towardes the east. Wash it till the oyle becomes white, and put it into the glass, and then put thereto the budds of hollyhocke, the flowers of maygolde the flowers or toppes of wild thyme, the budds of young hazle, and the thyme must be gathered near the side of a hill where fairies are use to be; and take the grasse of a fairy throne; then all these put into the glasse and set it to dissolve three days in the sunne and keep it for thy use.

Charm for a Barren Woman

Take an Hart's horne, turn into powder, and let it be mixed with a cow's gall; let a woman keepe it about her . . . and she shal conceive.

Throughout Europe, men and women sought all manner of charms to protect themselves from witchcraft, or simply to cure themselves of supposed bewitchment.

Among the pagan charms were anointing of the person with the gall of a crow, or the urine of a ram, or just sitting on a quill full of quicksilver. But the best charm of all against witches was considered to be that of suspending a tooth round the neck on a piece of cord—especially if the tooth had been plucked from the jaw of a hanged man while still suspended from the gallows. Among Christian charms, of which a favourite was the *Agnus Dei* (the 'Lamb of God' symbolised as a lamb supporting a banner), a design sometimes baked into the surface of a cake, were various symbolic candles, palms, crosses and small containers of salt (the symbol of immortality).

When accused of witchcraft at Lancaster, as Thomas Potts records in *The Trial of the Lancaster Witches* (1613), one Anne Whittle (Old Chattox) gave this charm as a sure cure for bewitching:

> Three Biters hast thou bitten,
> The Heart, ill Eye, ill Tongue;
> Three bitter shall be thy Boot,
> Father, Son and Holy Ghost
> a God's name.
> Five Pater-nosters, five Aves, and a Creed,
> In worship of five wounds of our Lord.

The trade in charms still flourishes today in all parts of Africa, the Bamucapi (witch-finders) of Malawi, for instance, offering protective charms against evil, snakes, pests and misfortunes at 17½p (42 cents) per cloth bag, or £5 ($ 12.00) for a potion guaranteed infallible in gaining the favour of government officers—always assuming they can be induced to drink it!

7

Cats and Demons, Toads and Weasels

Early man recognised a close link between himself and the animals which he used, feared and admired, so that in the course of time he devised magical rituals to obtain the powers of animals, and many were elevated to the realms of the supernatural. Today there are still many clues to this primitive man-animal mystic relationship. In South America, sorcerers have jaguar familiars which they affect to conjure up at will for divination, and in Africa witches are still believed to ride on hyenas at night, while in many parts of jungle Africa tribes are terrified by outbreaks of leopard men who, disguised in leopard regalia of mask and metal claws, kill their victims by piercing the jugular vein with the claws, and often practise cannibalism. It is not surprising, therefore, that witches of all ages have had their own magic menagerie.

> The witches have their spirits, some hath one, some hath more, as two, three, four and five, some in one likeness and some in another, as like cats, weasels, toads or mice, whom they nourish with milk or a chicken, or by letting them suck now and then a drop of blood.
>
> (George Gifford, *Dialogue Concerning Witches,* 1593)

The concept of the familiar, or familiar spirit, is *almost* exclusive to England and Scotland, where the theory was rife that, after a witch had made a contract with the Devil, he left behind some 'low demon' in animal form to advise her and perform small malicious errands, including murder. 'Each one of us', declared the Scottish witch Isobel Gowdie at her trial, 'has a spirit to wait upon us, when we please to call upon him.'

England's most fanatical witch-hunter, Matthew Hopkins, gives a classic account of witch familiars (*Discovery of Witches,* 1647) in the Elizabeth Clark case:

1. Holt, who came in like a white kitling (kitten).
2. Jamara, who came in like a fat spaniel without any legs at all. She said she kept him fat, for she (ie Elizabeth Clark) clapped her hand on her belly, and said he sucked good blood from her body.
3. Vinegar Tom, who was like a long-legged greyhound, with a head like an ox, with a long tail and broad eyes, who when this discoverer spoke to and bade him go to the place provided for him and his angels, immediately transformed himself into the shape of a child four years old without a head, and gave half a dozen turns about the house, and vanished at the door.
4. Sack and Sugar, like a black rabbit.
5. Newes, like a polecat.

While occasionally witches have hares, toads, crows and weasels in their entourage of familiars, the predominant animal is the cat. The association is not difficult to understand as, to the Ancient Egyptians, cats were considered sacred, and regarded as the incarnation of Isis, whose cat-headed daughter was called Bastet, or Pasht (hence Puss). Cats, too, were considered a symbol of fertility, while in medieval Aix-en-Provence, in France, a pagan cat ritual was preserved for decades in its entirety with the sanction of the Church. On Corpus Christi day a tom-cat was selected and wrapped in swaddling clothes (like the infant Jesus) and exhibited for public adoration. When, at noon, the sun traversed the meridian the wretched animal was ceremonially burnt alive; the custom being yet another adaptation of the classic pagan sacrifice of god-substitute (ie the sun-god dying by proxy so that he might rise again).

Sometimes the witches gave their cat familiars outlandish names like, Elemanzer, Pyewacket, Grizzel, Greedigut and Howffbacket.

In time, the chroniclers of past ages built up round the witches a whole host of attendant demons. Alphonsus de Spina (1467), one of their number, for instance, set down what he described as 'ten varieties of demons with which the witches consort':

> *Fates.* Some say they have seen Fates (cf, the three famous goddesses of Fate: Clotho, Lachesis and Atropos, who determined the birth, death and life of men), but if so they are not women but demons.
>
> *Poltergeists.* Commonly called the *duende de casa,* who do little tricks at night, like breaking things, pulling off bedclothes, making footsteps overheard. They move things but do little damage (the latter point is not supported by other writers on ghost phenomena).
>
> *Incubi* and *Succubi.* According to many theological texts, an *incubus* was an angel who fell from Heaven through lust for women, and nuns were said to be especially subject to these demons. The *succubus,* a demon in female form, specialised in seducing men. Caxton commented on both in his *Chronicle* 'Description of Wales':

That fiend that goth a-night
Women full oft to guile,
Incubus is named by right;
And guileth men other while,
Succubus is that wight.

When they (ie, the nuns) awake in the morning, they 'find themselves polluted as if they had slept with men'.

Marching hosts. These appear like hordes of men making much tumult.

Familiar demons. Those who eat and drink with men, in imitation of the angel of Tobit (one of the books of the Old Testament Apocrypha).

Nightmare demons. Evil spirits who terrify men in their dreams.

Demons formed from semen and its odour when men and women copulate. These demons also cause men to dream of women so the demons can 'receive their emission and make therefrom a new spirit'. (This is one demon in which Spina himself did not believe.)

Deceptive demons. Who appear sometimes as men and sometimes as women.

Clean demons. In fact, the foulest of demons who assail holy men.

Xorguinae or *bruxae.* Demons who deceive old women into thinking that they can fly to sabbats.

Another list, divided into the three hierarchies of a 'demon court' was compiled by Sebastian Michaëlis (see Index for other text references):

THE COURT OF DEMONS

Supreme Ruler: Lucifer

First Hierarchy: Primo principalis Belzebub (Adversary, St Francis), Chief of Seraphims.
Leviathan (Adversary, Peter the Apostle),

second only to Belzebub in the order of Seraphims, and who tempts men with sins that are directly repugnant to faith.

Asmodeus (Adversary, John the Baptist), the Seraphim Prince of Wantons.

Balberith, Prince of the Cherubim (Adversary, Barnabas), who tempts men to murder, contention and blasphemy.

Astaroth, Chief Prince of the order of Thrones (Adversary, Bartholomew), makes men desirous to sit idle and be slothful.

Verrine, second of Thrones (Adversary, Dominic), tempts men with impatience.

Gressil (Adversary, Bernard), third prince of the order of Thrones, tempts men with impurity and uncleanness.

Sonneillon (Adversary, Stephen), lowest prince of the order of Thrones, tempts men with hatred against their enemies.

Second Hierarchy: Oeillet, Prince of Dominions (Adversary, Martin), tempts monks to break the vow of poverty.

Rosier (Adversary, Basil), second in the order of Dominions, tempts by casting love spells.

Carreau (Adversary, Vincent), and Carnivean (Adversary, John the Evangelist), two demon princes of the order of Powers, who tempt by hardness of heart and obscenity respectively.

Verrier, Chief Prince of Principalities (Adversary, Bernard), tempts religious orders against the vow of obedience.

Third Hierarchy: In this hierarchy dwelt the princes of the order of Virtues, and archangels who drove men to cruelty, mercilessness and arrogance over the poor. Ruled by Belias, Olivier and Iuvart, who could only be overcome by uttering prayers written by their mortal enemies, Francis de Paul, and Lawrence.

One demon particularly feared by the witches themselves was *mare* (quite distinct from the term 'mare', meaning a female horse), who would come upon a sleeper during the night and, by sitting on the chest, cause feelings of suffocation.

8

Portrait of a Witch's Garden

An essential part of witchcraft lore is a knowledge of the properties of herbs, flowers, fungi and trees, both magical and medicinal, which was once called 'wort-cunning'.

The coupling of this herb-lore with the preparation of magic potions in a cauldron is both traditional and symbolic, the hollow vessel having obvious female associations and signifying the very Womb of Nature in which all kinds of magic could be conceived. The three legs of the cauldron also symbolised the triple Moon goddess, the patronness of witches.

Added to the symbolism of the cauldron were the four main elements of life; *fire*, to heat the cauldron; *water*, to fill it; the fruits of the *earth* to prepare in it; and the pungent steam from it rising into the *air* and providing a medium in which clairvoyants might claim to see the wavering shapes of future happenings.

The main plants in a witch's garden were generally held to be as follows:

MONK'S HOOD, or Wolf's Bane, produced the much sought-after poison aconite (the poison of 'Romeo and Juliet'), which was originally deemed to have sprung from the saliva of Cerberus, the fierce three-headed god of the Greek underworld, Hades. All parts of the plant are poisonous.

HENBANE (*Hyoscyamus*, derivative hyoscine), another effective poison used by witches. Known to Plutarch, henbane was generally woven by witches into a head ornament for the dead against evil influences, but today, as in ancient times, it is used for horse disorders. Preparations made from the leaf of this narcotic poison were used by witches both in Europe and the United States, where growths flourish.

WILLOW BARK (nicknamed 'witch's asprin' because it contains acetylsalicylic acid) was a powerful witch remedy against rheumatism.

HEMLOCK (*Conium maculatum*) was used in the form both of the leaves and fruit. A paralysing agent, the poison was administered to Socrates. Sometimes this drug was mixed with green frog's bones, wolf's tail hair, or cat's brains for extra potency, but the old witch recipes are not clear as to the specific purpose.

DEADLY NIGHTSHADE (*Atropa belladonna*) with its active principle of atropine, the juice of the deadly nightshade, was used by witches to stimulate visions.

SELAGO (*Lycopodium clavatum*, or *Lycopodium selago*) is a fine yellow powder, comprising the spores of the club-moss and was used by witches to enable them to understand the language of birds and beasts. Perhaps the Druids were the first to use it, but only if it had been gathered on a moonlight, cloudless night by a naked maiden.

DATURA, a genus of plants, of which *Datura stramonium*, or thorn-apple, has strong narcotic properties. These were used to produce frenzied delirium in which victims would dance themselves to death. Another powerful stimulant which drove people to dance was masterwort (*imperatoria ostruthium*), usually mixed into a beverage.

ST JOHN'S WORT (*Hypericum*), boiled in wine, was a popular witch remedy against vomiting blood. According to superstition, the red spots on this plant make their appearance on 29 August, the day of St John's beheading.

Herbs and flowers for protection against sorcery included: verbena, cyclamen, pimpernel, angelica, bracken, fern, broom, maidenhair, ground ivy, fennel, garlic and agrimony. As an old verse says:

> Trefoil, vervain, St John's wort and Dill
> Hinder all witches of their foul will.

MANDRAKE (*Mandragora podophyllum*) is a plant around which many mysteries have been collected. Basically a narcotic plant whose roots often grow into the shape of human limbs, it is mentioned in the Bible as the ingredient for love philtres and in Greek legend as the Plant of Circe, enchantress of the island of Aeaea who was consulted by Odysseus.

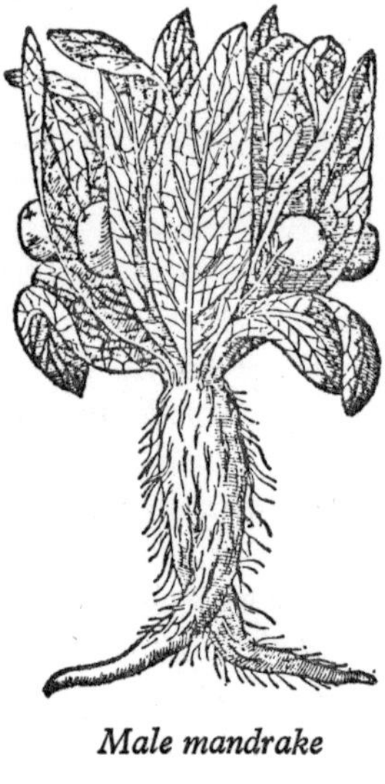

Male mandrake

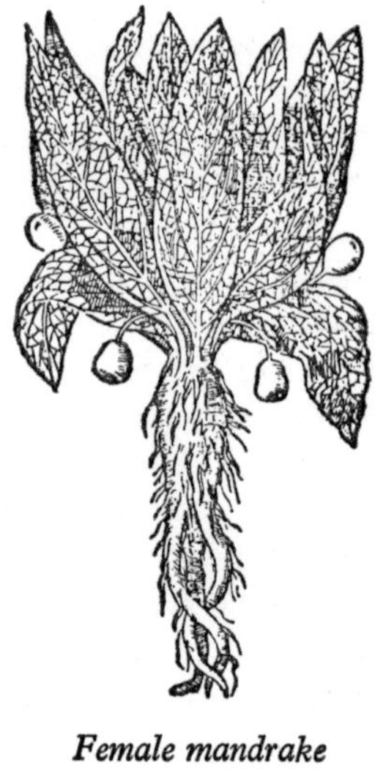

Female mandrake

As mentioned in the book *Strange and Wondrous Plants*, mandrake was deemed 'to grow under the gallows of hanged men—pulled from the ground the root emitted wild shrieks, and those who heard them were driven mad'. In my *Book of Superstitions* (David & Charles/Taplinger Publishing Co., 1970), it was noted how the root was sometimes collected in ancient times:

> No man ever pulled its bifurcated roots himself if he could possibly help it, and one way of collecting it was to tie a hungry dog to the plant, after the soil round the roots had been loosened with an ivory or iron tool. With a piece of food placed just outside its reach, the dog would strain and eventually pull the mandrake out of the earth. Meanwhile the gatherer had retired out of earshot, for the mandrake was thought to utter a death-curse as it left the earth. After a while, the gatherer would return to untie the mandrake from the dog's harness, and many are the stories of dogs who were found dead beside the uprooted mandrake.

The mandrake was often used by witches in potions to increase sexual powers, using the 'male' or 'female' roots where relevant. The whole class of herbs such as mandrake, nightshade, henbane and so on, was entitled the *Solanaceae*, 'the herbs of consolation'.

FOXGLOVE, the source of digitalis, was named not after foxes but after 'Folk's Glove', the glove of the 'good folk', or fairies. The medicinal properties of foxglove were first discovered by the witches, but were brought into 'reputable medicine' by one William Withering, a doctor who lived in Shropshire during the eighteenth century. The old story goes that Withering noticed that an old witch was able to cure people of dropsy (an abnormal accumulation of fluid beneath the skin, or in one or more of the cavities of the body) by dosing them with herbal tea. He purchased her recipe and discovered that its most important ingredient was foxglove.

Withering became famous through this discovery, and his

epitaph in Edgbaston Old Church, Birmingham, is ornamented with carvings of foxglove. Nor was he by any means the first to use witch remedies to good effect. The famous mystic and alchemist Philippus Aureolus Paracelsus (1493–1541), for example, was another who was never too proud to learn medicine from a witch.

The actual time of collecting these magical herbs was held to be vitally important, and the correct phase of the moon had to be calculated before harvesting. As the witches understood it, the waxing of the moon was the time for constructive magic, and its waning for destructive legerdemain or banishment. Witches also thought it necessary to use a magical number of herbs in a spell or potion; either three, seven or nine different herbs being the most common multiples used.

Not all witches' herb potions were made into liquids in a cauldron, some were powdered and sewn into small sachets as charms. Here is the recipe for such herb charm from Scotland, by which a woman might attract a lover:

> Pick to attract thy lover vervain, southernwood and fragrant orris root. Crush between sandstone and sew into a small purse, using emerald green silk the dress of Venus; sew on a Friday in the increase of the moon and pin inside the clothes next to the skin.

ORRIS ROOT (found mostly in the south of Europe) was used by witches for divination. The method was to tie a thread round the 'neck' of the root, often shaped like a seated human figure, and thence the root was held like a pendulum. A wish was then made, or a question asked by the diviner, who would then wait and concentrate on which way the root moved. An affirmative answer was forecast if the root moved *deasil* (clockwise) and negative if *widdershins* (anti-clockwise). Should the root swing only from side to side, the answer was deemed uncertain. Usually this divination was conducted at night by the light of a wax candle.

Witches also took great care in the layout of their magic plots. The central point of the garden had to be a tree (of any type other than rowan) around which was planted a circle of white flowers to honour the Moon goddess. Sometimes, for extra power, a stone or wooden figure of a unicorn was placed with its horn pointing towards the tree. A lemon tree was particularly favoured, as it was said to bring news and messages of all kinds (hence its dedication to Hermes, Greek god of Mercury and of couriers), and to promote mental and manual dexterity.

A WITCH'S FLORA CHART

As witches believed that matter could exude magic emanations, the effect of which on people varied in intensity according to their birth date, they evolved a flora chart (see page 94).

Consulting her almanac, the witch would choose flowers to plant so that from January (snowdrops) to December (Christmas roses) she would have some colour in her garden to help her raise the power. Golden and orange flowers and blossoms, sacred to Apollo, seem to have predominated in the witches' gardens, perhaps as a symbol of the sun, while a corner was always found for a thistle or two, the stimulants of vitality.

A witch's front rank of defence against ill-wishers was three or four rows of red flowers, nicknamed 'witch soldiers'; these serried ranks of geraniums, pelargoniums, nasturtiums and red-hot pokers, in occult hues of red and flame, were said to keep the witch-hunters at bay.

Some witches planted in consultation with the Zodiac and thus cultivated on Sunday for the Sun, Monday for the Moon, Tuesday for Mars, Wednesday for Mercury, Thursday for Jupiter and Neptune, Friday for Venus, and Saturday for Saturn and Uranus. When money was needed, the colour purple was held to be most propitious for invocation, and so clumps of purple flowers like purple violets, irises, sorcerer's periwinkle, and the overhanging lilac were always to be found in a witch's garden.

If there was a well in a witch's garden, nearby would be

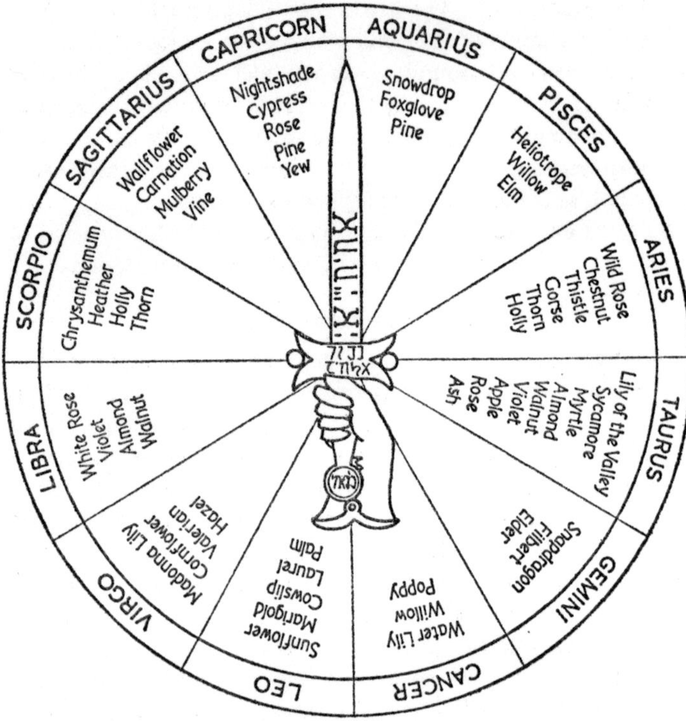

A witch's flora chart

found a 'wheel of fortune', improvised perhaps from a discarded cartwheel. The witch would step out the magic nine paces from the well and there set up the wheel, which she would bedeck with blue morning glories to ensure harmony in her own household, where cats, toads, dogs and weasels had to live amicably with the other legions of 'familiars'.

Certain weeds were encouraged to grow, for each had its own occult power, and to complete her garden the witch placed near the gate a multicoloured rank of anemonies to give her warning by their movements of the approach of strangers.

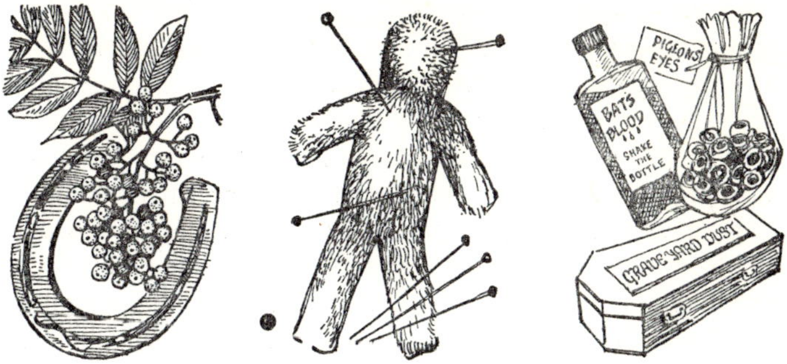

9

Credulity and Superstition

The widespread belief in witchcraft naturally prompted an assiduous search for effective means of protection against the evil powers of witches, and a number of these talismans and protective customs are to be found enshrined in folk-lore in many parts of the world.

Anything made of iron or steel (especially horseshoes) is still highly regarded as a witch repellent, but perhaps, above all others, salt has always been believed to be the most powerful deterrent. Incorruptible in itself and with power to preserve other things from decay, salt soon became the emblem of immortal life and eternity, and was widely used to keep away witches. Dairymaids dropped a pinch of it into their pails before milking, and buttermakers did the same with their churns to ward off witches, whose evil influence could be most harmful when milk was just 'on the turn'.

In the Outer Hebrides of Scotland, cattle were rubbed with

salt before being moved from one pasture to another, and fishermen of the river Tweed (on the borders of England and Scotland) sprinkled their nets and boats for the same reason, to deter the harmful attentions of witches.

A very ancient superstition was that a newborn baby was most prone to 'witching', and mothers were earnestly counselled by the wise to wear a garment with three parallel slits cut somewhere in the fabric, to serve as a 'drain' for evil influences. It was also commonly believed that witches frequently attempted to prevent delivery, one of their methods being to make or tighten knots before or during a woman's labour. Thus any competent midwife, as soon as she arrived on the scene, would make sure that all the knots in the neighbourhood of the delivery bed were loosened.

Methods of identifying witches were legion and varied from country to country but two were generally held to be particularly effective. First, it was believed that the innocence or guilt of a suspected witch could be determined by secretly driving a long nail into her footprint. If the suspect were indeed a witch, she would be compelled by the power of the metal burning into the sole of her foot to return and draw the nail out; if innocent, she would be untroubled by the nail.

The second method was the age-old custom of 'touching the victim'. Thomas Potts, in *The Wonderfull Discoverie of Witches in the Countie of Lancaster* (1613), describes how, when Jennet Preston was tried at York for the murder by witchcraft of Thomas Lister, she was forced to touch his body, which bled as soon as she laid hands on it. Which circumstance Potts explained, 'hath euer beene held a great argument to induce a Iurie to hold him guiltie that shall be accused of Murther, and hath seldome, or neuer, fayled in the Tryall'.

Three trees most commonly asociated with witches are the hazel, the elder and the rowan. A holy tree from Celtic times, the hazel was much favoured for the making of rods to detect the presence of water or metal in the earth, and though witches were sometimes 'diviners', they also used hazel rods to point at a victim and so increase their power over him. Many Scottish children, particularly those born in the autumn, were once given the 'milk' of the hazel fruit mixed with honey as their first food, as an antidote to witch 'overlooking'.

The elder was once considered the unluckiest of all woods to bring into the house; even today folk in Shropshire believe that to do so will cause a death among the occupying family within twelve months. Nor should a baby's cradle ever be made of elder wood, for this would attract witches who would rock it so violently as to injure the child within. And if, when an elder tree was felled, a profuse amount of sap issued from the severed end, its wood would not be used for building or carpentry as this secretion was thought to be a sure sign of witch possession.

The rowan, or mountain ash, was considered a fortunate tree indeed, with power to avert witchcraft, disease and the ubiquitous Evil Eye. 'Rowan tree and red thread gar the witches tyne their speed', was a well-known saying in Scotland, where a house was given extra protection by tying with red thread crosses of rowan twigs above the lintel of a door. It was also extensively planted in Scottish graveyards to keep away witches and warlocks, and one famous rowan-protected grave is that of David Ritchie of Woodhouse, familiarly known as 'Bowed Davie o' the Wuddus'. A dwarf, only 3½ft tall, Davie became a celebrity when Sir Walter Scott, who had met him in 1797, chose him as a prototype for his novel *The Black Dwarf*. Davie's last wish was that his grave be protected from witches and so it can be seen today at Manor Churchyard, Peeblesshire.

One very persistent superstition was that a witch's power could be destroyed by the letting of her blood; 'scoring above the breath' therefore was a common practice in the heyday of witch belief. The witch's blood was drawn by scratching her above the nose or mouth, a practice once indulged in by angry mob and village constables alike.

A particularly unpleasant affliction of mankind for which

witches were often blamed was the 'sendyng of lice aupone ane cleane personie', and in 1645 Alice Warner, of Rushmere, Suffolk, confessed that she had sent lice to plague two women who had offended her. Her official deposition, a document which may still be seen at the British Museum in London, records in conclusion that 'the sd women were lousie, according as she confessed'.

Dew collected on the morning of May Day was considered as potent for good as for evil and in his *Notes on the Folk-Lore of the Northern Counties of England and the Borders* (1879), William Henderson records how two Scottish witches were seen brushing May dew from the grass of a field with a hair-tether. When they had finished, the tether was taken from them and hung in the neighbouring cowbyre, after which the cows gave so much milk that there were not enough containers in the vicinity to hold it. In the south-eastern parts of Europe, however, cattle were rubbed with dew on May Day morn to free them from the perils of witchcraft throughout the coming year.

Owls have always been associated with witchcraft, their feathers and bones being most often used in spells. In *Macbeth*, the witches used an owlet's wing 'for a charm of powerful trouble', and in Horace's writings (*Epode*, V, 15, 16) a screech-owl's feathers are mentioned as part of a witch's brew. Owl broth, incidentally, was once given to children in England who suffered from whooping cough.

Superstition, too, laid milk-stealing at the door of witches, who were deemed able to milk cows from a distance, and among the charms used to prevent this were a rowan stick thrust through the animal's tail hair, or a special tether made from horsehair.

Clothes of all kinds had to be kept out of a witch's way in case she cursed them and thereby their owners when they next put them on, and personal names were kept secret from strangers lest an unsuspected witch might use the constituent letters to cast a damning spell. For the same reason, people also took care when cutting their finger-nails or hair to destroy the shorn tufts and parings.

In *Dialect and Folk-Lore of Northamptonshire* (1851), T. Sternberg records a curiously simple method by which a devotee of magic could become a witch by just trimming the finger-nails; all that had to be done was to sit by the hearth and cut the nails while reciting, 'I wish I was as far from God as my nails are far from dirt.'

Superstitions about witchcraft are still current today, and some actors will have nothing to do with the Shakespearian play *Macbeth*, because of its associations with witchcraft. Stories abound of how mysterious accidents, outbreaks of fire and so on, occurred at certain theatres when the play was running, and some even attribute the death in 1937 of the famous manager of the Old Vic and Sadler's Wells, Lilian Mary Baylis, to the fact that *Macbeth* was playing at the time.

And in Italy in 1969, when Raffaeli Minichiello was imprisoned by the US authorities for hi-jacking an air-liner, newspapers reported that the villagers of his native Melito Irpino, in the hills above Naples, were getting up a subscription to engage a witch to rescue him by mystic transference from the hands of the FBI in New York!

10

Witches in the Modern World

Except for the celebrated Osborn case of 1751, in which Ruth Osborn, a suspected witch, was beaten to death by a mob, the period from 1736 (following the repeal of James I's Act) to 1850 saw less public concern about witches in Britain, although witchcraft was still practised underground and belief in its existence never died out.

In 1801 there was published in London *The Magus, or Celestial Intelligencer; Being a Complete System of Occult Philosophy* (republished 1967, University Books, New York), written by Francis Barrett and containing vivid portraits of demons. Very little is known about Barrett, but it is thought that he taught magic to paying pupils, although his knowledge of the subject as revealed in his writings appears to be less than profound, his *Magus* being more or less a rehash of the text of the early magical books, called *grimoires*. Nevertheless, it may have been Barrett who instigated the fashion amongst the gentry to study the occult, offering a little black amongst white magic; as Barrett himself records, 'I have, in the country, by only speaking a few words, and used other things, caused terrible rains and claps of thunder.'

The real renaissance of modern witchcraft, however, was more probably due to Eliphas Levi (1810–75), a French Roman Catholic priest who practised the ancient magic arts as a side-line. Levi became acquainted with an English occult group led by Bulwer Lytton (1803–73), a prolific novelist and dramatist, and revealed his practices to them. Soon, other societies sprang up and, following Levi's example, practised magic and witchcraft, both black and white, taking in healing, divination, self-preferment, and even ritual murder. Then there appeared upon the scene a far more sinister figure, born Edward Alexander Crowley, at 30 Clarendon Square, Leamington, Warwickshire, in the last hour of 12 October 1875.

Later to be known as Aleister Crowley, he remains perhaps the most remarkable, in terms of degeneracy, and at the same time the most sinister figure of the twentieth century. An eminent scholar, he turned his intellect to the art of witchcraft and during his early twenties joined the Society of the Golden Dawn, of which the Irish lyric poet and dramatist William Butler Yates (1865–1939) was also a member, and became a self-proclaimed magician.

Such was his mastery of the black arts that to many Crowley became the embodiment of evil, and his unholy rites and orgiastic ceremonies shocked even the most hardened cynics. Described by the international press of the 1920s as 'A Man We'd like to Hang', 'The Wickedest Man in the World', and 'The King of Depravity', Crowley made a mockery of the traditional laws of witchcraft and died in 1947, thoroughly loathed by the public at large.

A contemporary of Crowley's, and perhaps the man who most influenced the revival of practical witchcraft in England in this century, was a retired civil servant, Gerald Brosseau Gardner

(1884–1964). Gardner claimed to have been initiated into the first grade of witchcraft by a group of witches who practised in the New Forest, and from this beginning he proceeded to recruit so many covens of his own that 'Gardnerian' witches became a recognised cult. Gardner later became director of the Museum of Magic and Witchcraft at the Witches' Mill, Castletown, Isle of Man.

In his book *Witchcraft Today* (Rider, 1954; Jarrolds, 1968), Gardner expressed the opinion that witches worshipped a Horned God and a Mother Goddess, and that modern witches cast spells for good, to heal the sick and propagate good crops. He further claimed that the witches extant today were direct heirs of those who had been burned during the Middle Ages. His second book, *The Meaning of Witchcraft* (Rider, 1959; Jarrolds, 1968), further reiterated his ideas concerning the 'healthy' nature of the religion of 'Wicca' which, as a cult, he contended dated from pre-Christian times.

By the time Gardner died in 1964 there were covens of Gardnerian witches in many parts of Britain. Their members came from all strata of society and though their rites were said to include nude ceremonial, flagellation, and ritualistic copulation, these modern believers in the 'Old Religion' were held to be comparatively harmless and to have little or nothing to do with what press reports call the 'churchyard vandalism' type of magic.

Most British witches seem to be lapsed members of the Christian faith, who believe that Christianity is outmoded or has failed in some way to come to terms with modern living. To such, Gardner's theories on witchcraft could no doubt prove attractive, as were those of the late Dr Margaret Murray who believed witchcraft to be a survival of the pagan religions of Europe. While Murray's ideas are not accepted by most historians, Britain's witches give them prominence in their philosophy.

Two characteristics seem to identify modern British witches:

their love of ceremony and their inherent schismatic tendencies.

In 1969 there was published a book, *King of the Witches* (Peter Davies, London), written by a British journalist, June Johns. It tells the allegedly true story of one Alex Sanders, a self-proclaimed 'professional' white witch who, as a seven-year old child, was initiated into the witch cult by his grandmother. Sometime in 1965, as reputed head of over 100 covens, Sanders was elected 'King of the Witches', a title last held in the fifteenth century by Owain Glendwr, the last independent Prince of Wales, and though they follow diverse customs, the Sanders sect of witches is probably the best organised one in Britain to-day. The sudden spread of semi-organised witch groups dates from the publication of Margaret Murray's *Witchcraft in Western Europe* and *The God of the Witches.*

Next to Britain, Germany would appear to be the European country which has seen the greatest revival of interest in witch-craft, although some may consider this to be only an extension of racialism. Not long ago mob violence was reported in Franconia, a somewhat backward Bavarian Catholic peasant province, against a half-crazed old *hausfrau* accused of bewitching her neighbour. The accusation took the traditional form. Her neighbour's best cow had died mysteriously, lice had infested his house, his well had dried up and his wife had miscarried. It may or may not be significant that Adolf Hitler's fanatical Jew-baiter and lecher, Julius Streicher, was once Gauleiter of Franconia, and exploited old witch-hunting instincts by accusing local Jews of witchcraft practices. In their absence, it could be that peasants might be tempted to seek out the traditional old woman on whom to vent their spite.

An interesting sidelight on modern witchcraft is the extent to which Europe's once widespread belief in it is still found reflected in children's games. A common game in many parts of Europe is 'witch's tig': a chaser is chosen and his or her task is to run after the other players, when one has been caught he is 'touched' and rendered 'bewitched'. The touched player must then stand upright where he is with arms outstretched until another player 'releases' him with a counter-touch; all the time the bewitched one can shout to the other players to come and release him. Meanwhile, the chaser attempts to catch the other players and likewise transfix them. The game ends when the chaser manages to catch all the players, or until one player has been caught twice. The game is known severally as 'cats and witches' (Spalding, Lincolnshire), 'witches' tag' (Belfast, Nothern Ireland), *Hexe geh hexe steh* (Berlin, Germany), (*Versteinern, Steinern Hex, or Erlbsen* (Austria), and *Strega che impala,* or *Incantesimo* (Italy).

In another game, played mostly by girls, a chaser runs after the other players and when she catches one places her in a 'witch's gluepot'. Before the game starts, the 'witch' marks out a circle or chooses a place where her 'gluepot' is to be (a corner, a gateway and so on). Once caught and placed in the 'gluepot', the victim must remain until released by another player. American children play a similar game called 'Witch in the Jar', and in Germany it is called *Die Hexe.*

According to researchers at the University of South Carolina more and more young people are turning to black magic and witchcraft every year. The world-wide publicity given to the trial of Charles Manson, the hippy leader accused in the Sharon Tate murder case, is said to have stimulated new interest in the occult and, to quote Dr Robert Ellwood, Professor of Religion at the University of South Carolina: 'The Manson case is a good example of how young people are abandoning traditional religions in favour of unconventional ones.'

In the United States, too, there is an increasing demand among children for toys associated with the occult, astrology and witchcraft—one popular set is stamped 'Made in Witch City' (reputed to be somewhere in California).

Shops selling witch paraphernalia have existed in New York since the middle of the nineteenth century and even today all-purpose witch kits, DUME (death unto mine enemy) hexing candles at seventy-five cents each, bat's blood, pigeon's eyes and graveyard dust bring in for their salesmen an estimated $2,500,000 per year. Most witch supply centres are to be found in the Negro-and Spanish-speaking neighbourhoods of New York, and Voodoo shops in particular, called *botanicas,* are to be found huddled around New York's markets at 116th Street and Park Avenue, Harlem, their windows stacked with gaudily painted madonnas, plastic herb charms and portable evil eyes. An undoubted best-seller is a hexing doll, complete with a packet of twelve extra long pins, all for $2.50.

So powerful is this witch material alleged to be that, not long ago, a Manhattan court granted a divorce to a woman who claimed that her husband had tried to bewitch her by sprinkling graveyard dust in her salad dressing.

And in the witch districts of modern New York they have a saying: 'Rich folks go to headshrinkers (psychiatrists) with their troubles, poor folk consult witches.'

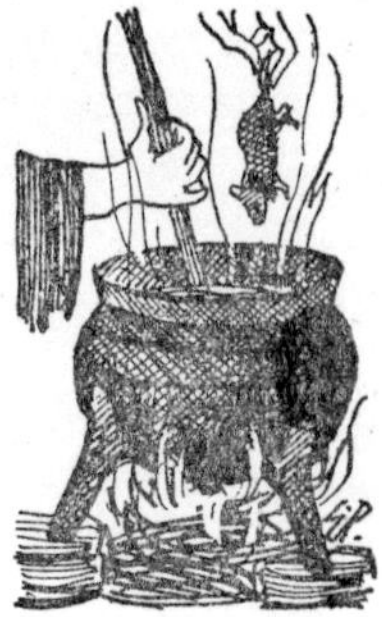

II

The Language of the Witches

Those who extend their studies into the history, folk art and practice of witchcraft will come across several obscure and abstruse references. Here is a paragraph or two on some of the most common words and references used in modern witchcraft.

ANGELS

In the language of magic, such angels are not the winged apparitions of Christian lore, nor are they souls of the dead in visual form, but spirits drawn from the central source of power in the universe. Witches and magicians alike believe that these 'angels' may be petitioned to advise and help mortals who carry out the appropriate rituals.

ATHAME (or ARTHAME)

The witches' black-handled magic knife, used for drawing the magic circle. Used by modern witches still, the blade and handle of the athame bear magic symbols. (Cf the *ad-adhamme*, a ritual knife used by the magicians of Berber tribes.)

BOOK OF SHADOWS

This is the basic manual of witchcraft containing the charts, recipes and instructions for the various magic rites. Almost unaltered over the years, the book must be copied out in a witch's own handwriting, so that if arrested no other witch but herself would be implicated.

Here are some extracts from the laws of witchcraft as given in the *Book of Shadows*:

> The Wicca (ancient word for witchcraft) should give due worship to the gods and obey their will, which they ordain, for it was made for the good of Wicca as the worship of Wicca is good for the gods. For the gods love the brethren of Wicca. . . .
>
> And it is necessary that the Circle which is the temple of the gods, should be truly cast and purified. And that it may be a fit place for the gods to enter. . . .
>
> For in this way only may men have communion with the gods, for the gods cannot help man without the help of man. . . .
>
> Let each high-priestess govern her coven (group of witches—covenstead is the place where witches meet) with justice and love, with the help and advice of the high-priest and the elders, always heeding the advice of the messenger of the gods if he cometh. . . .
>
> The Brotherhood is powerful and will help you to escape if you stand fast, but if you betray ought there is no hope for you in this life or in that to come. . . .
>
> Never boast, never threaten, never say you would wish ill of anyone. . . .
>
> If it is not possible to achieve your ends one way, perchance the aim may be achieved by acting in a different way

so as to harm none. *May the curse of the Goddess be upon any who breaketh this law.* So be it ordained. . . .

BLACK MASS

Black Mass is a colourful term which commonly appears in newspaper reports of witch practices, but has little meaning. Black Mass is really the romantic concept of diabolism which became fashionable in certain elegant circles during the 1890s. Aleister Crowley and his forerunners set out with the avowed intention of worshipping Satan (or to appear to do so) and their Black Mass was a deliberate parody of Christian rites. The basic concept of deliberately parodying the Christian Mass seems to date only from the eighteenth century as a literary invention of the Marquis de Sade (Count Donatien Alphonse François Sade; see *Justine,* 1791) who, as a freak of a decadent society, introduced to the jaded élite the sophisticated perversion that deliberate Satanism is.

FITH-FATH

Near to the end of the reign of the XX Dynasty Pharaoh Rameses III (1182–1151 BC), a princess called Tiye decided that if her supporters got rid of Rameses III and the sons of Queen Isis (the great royal wife, whose eldest son had been chosen as hereditary prince), her own son Pentawere might ascend the throne. Aided and abetted by two palace functionaries, certain magic practices were undertaken against the Pharaoh, which included the making of wax images to the accompaniment of magic incantations.

Eventually the culprits were arrested and paid the capital penalty of illicit magic, but the idea of making wax images for derogative sympathetic magic began to take hold, strengthened no doubt by the fact that Rameses III had died before the trial started. From Ancient Egypt, the superstitious use of wax images, to be called *fith-faths,* passed to Greece and Rome, and thence from classical times to general use in Europe.

One of the clearest accounts of waxen images was given by Mother Demdike at the trial of the Lancashire Witches in 1612:

> The speediest way to take a man's life away by witchcraft is to make a picture (figurine) of clay, like unto the shape of the person whom they mean to kill and dry it thoroughly. And when you would have them to be ill in any one place more than another, then take a thorn or pin and prick it in that part of the picture you would have to be ill. And when you would have any part of that body to consume away, then take that part of the picture and burn it. And so thereupon by that means the body shall die. . . .

Thomas Hardy, in *The Return of the Native* (1878), also gives a classic example of wax image magic as practised in the nineteenth century. In the story, Susan Nonesuch, fearing that an evil spell has been cast on her son by Eustacia Yeobright, uses a 'fith-fath' as a counter-action.

KEY OF SOLOMON

An Ancient Hebrew book of magic and one of the few storehouses of witchcraft to have come down through the ages in its almost original form. It contains charts and a wide selection of pentacles and elaborate Hebrew symbols. (As with the *Book of Shadows*, this volume is very rare, but a copy is to be found in the John Rylands Library, Manchester.)

LAMIA

A common Latin word to describe a witch; in classical legend, Lamia was Queen of Libya and beloved of Zeus.

MAYA

A witch name meaning 'Mother Goddess'.

SABBAT

The major meeting of a whole coven, or several covens is

called a sabbat; two great, or grand sabbats are frequently mentioned in history. The first reputedly took place as a result of the Spanish Armada being sighted on 29 July 1588 (19 July, OS) by Capt Thomas Fleming, of the bark *Golden Hind.* News of the impending clash of England and Spain spread quickly and the witches of the time gathered in secret covens to conjure up a north-westerly gale to cripple the Spanish ships. To mark the occasion, many wore the medallion with the inscription, *Afflavit Deus et Dissipantur*—'God has sent forth his breath and they are dispersed'.

While some witches are thought to have gathered to misdirect Napoleon Bonaparte's attempt to invade England, the next great sabbat is said to have been held during World War II, when some 400 witches gathered in the New Forest (Hampshire) to raise enough magic power to keep Hitler away from Britain's coasts. To increase the power, some of the witches volunteered to be ritualistically scourged. Later, when mist and fog obscured the English Channel and the projected invasion (Operation 'Sea Lion') was postponed indefinitely, the witches not unnaturally claimed that their petition had been answered.

SORCERY

Harmful magic; *in the main* the sorcerer uses material objects while a witch does not.

WARLOCK

Originally the warlock was the witch who bound the initiate, but today the term is used by *non-witches* to describe a male witch.

WHISPERING RUNES

The letters used in the northern part of Europe in the early centuries AD were considered powerful magic. Called runes, the root of the word originally meant 'mystery, secret'; it now survives in the modern German word *raunen,* 'to whisper', although scholars agree that some of the runes derive from Greek and Latin.

Originally, runes were carved on such objects as jewels, swords and furniture to keep away evil, but several tombs have their runic inscriptions to keep away dark forces from the dead. Part of the rune inscription of the Björkertorpstone, in Sweden, reads, 'This is the meaning of the runes; I hid here magic runes undisturbed by evil witchcraft. He who destroys this monument shall die in misery by magic art.'

The ancient poem called *Havamal* (Utterance of the High One) goes further to say that runes have power to bring the dead to life:

> A twelfth (spell) I know; when I see aloft upon a tree
> A corpse swinging from a rope
> Then I cut and paint runes
> So that the man walks
> And speaks with Me.

Index